The Universe Doesn't Give A Sh*t About Your Book

A Brutally Honest Guide To Self-Publishing

E. Rachael Hardcastle

ISBN: 978-1-9999688-4-7

Cover design & formatting: E. Rachael Hardcastle

For permission requests, write to the publisher at the address below.

Curious Cat Books
PO Box 348, Shipley, BD189ER, United Kingdom

www.erachaelhardcastle.com
www.curiouscatbooks.co.uk

First Edition

Printed by Ingramspark

The Universe Doesn't Give A Sh*t About Your Book

E. Rachael Hardcastle

Other Titles By E. Rachael Hardcastle

Fiction

Finding Pandora: The Complete Collection

Noah Finn & the Art of Suicide

Aeon Infinitum: Run For Your Life

Bluetooth & the World Wide Web

Forgotten Faith

Non-Fiction

The Universe Doesn't Give A Sh*t About Your Book

What's In This Thing, Anyway?

Introduction

Read Me!

Before you do anything else, please read and remember the below. You're not going to like it, but you need to hear it. I apologise in advance.

In fact, no I don't—I take it back.

It's better to hear this now and from someone who wants you to succeed and is rooting for you, than some a-hole.

Ready?

Brace yourself...

The universe doesn't give a sh*t about your book—that's the truth. Something you create is always going to mean more to you than anyone else, so before you start your self-publishing 'journey', try to remember that.

A lack of sales and interest in something you've produced is nothing personal, though sometimes it can certainly feel that way. If your book is finished and ready to publish, you'll know exactly how difficult writing is and how close to your heart your story has become. You've spent months (perhaps even years) worrying and spending time perfecting it. For someone to shoot it down in the first week of its existence will be painful.

Some people will provide you with feedback in a not-so-friendly manner, regardless of how much effort you've put into the book or how nice you've been to them. So, 1* reviews are a possibility you can't avoid, nor should you try, because everyone is entitled to their opinion and you can't please some no matter what you do. Even if 90% think it's the best thing they've discovered since sliced bread, 10% might think it's sh*t. And you know what, they might be right.

If you're still writing (or are yet to start) and are reading this book to prepare for what's to come, then what I'm about to say now applies to you.

Self-publishing is generally not a big money-making business and it can be a very lonely job. That's not to say you won't become a huge success or rich from your writing because there are plenty of great examples out there who make a living from it. However, writing is a solitary hobby for most, even if they have a co-author because there will come a time when what's in your mind needs to meet paper, and only *you* will know how to do that because only *you* can access your thoughts.

Of course, there are lots of things every writer needs to prepare themselves to hear. Some are daft, some are offensive and some—well, some you don't even have to entertain. Here are a few examples (and no doubt the response you've often dreamt of giving!):

- **'So you're not '*published published*' then?'**

  - What even *is* 'published published'? Do you mean my book isn't real because a big house didn't sign me?

- **'You don't want to do this full time, do you? You're not serious about this writing business, are you? Can't you just get a proper job?'**

  - Actually yes, I'm pretty serious about this 'writing business'. I have another job, so if you think about it, I'm actually working *two* now, thank you very much.

- **'Can I read your book? It's free, right? Will you send me a copy?'**

  - Yes, you can read it and no, you can't have it for free!

- **'Why are you stressing over this? It's just a hobby!'**

  - You don't even have to answer that. You have my permission to smile and nod, then politely leave the room.

- **'How hard can writing be? I was thinking about writing a book, but I don't have time.'**

  - Hmm, I don't have anything else pressing going on in my life, either, so I write to fill the void in my soul. I'm a writer, so it's mostly dark in there anyway...

- **'Are you done yet?'**

  - No, I'll be finished when I'm finished. Sod off.

Like me, I'm sure you have never responded to any of those daft statements and questions in that manner out loud, nor should you. Let's be professional here. What goes on inside your head is your business and if you want to curse them later in the comfort of your own home, by all means have at it. But in the meantime, just offer a well-rehearsed, friendly response and keep working hard to achieve your writing and publishing dreams.

Each to their own.

Just remember to smile.

Disclaimer

I want you to take what I say on board but with a pinch of

salt. I am *one* writer. I am *one* reader. I am *one* publisher. And, as you know, there are many, many others. Therefore, I can only give you *my* opinion and advise you based on *my* experiences and the knowledge I've gained through research and practices. What I tell you in this book is also based on how I have interpreted the advice of others—the more mentors you can find, the better.

It's up to you how much of this you apply to your own 'journey' (ooh, I *hate* that phrase but it fits what I'm trying to say here), and how right or wrong you think I am. Until you read about my life as an author, I'm one less mentor you can learn from—the more people you speak to, the better you can decide for yourself what works and what doesn't.

I'm not a lawyer and I've never worked in a large publishing house. So, with regards to contracts and agreements and outsourcing jobs like editing and cover design etc., you may want to seek professional guidance from someone qualified. I have, however, had training with regards copy-editing and self-publishing. Plus, I've always been an avid reader and for several years designed covers and formatted manuscripts for authors all over the world.

I've been an indie author since 2010, but writing in general for much longer. My debut novel was released at 18 years old, but I got my first recognition as a writer at just 14 years for an inspirational poem I wrote (which was, *technically,* the first thing I ever had published!).

How to use this book, and the stuff I'm assuming...

I do a lot of assuming in this book.

'*When you assume, you make an ass out of u and me*'.

Sorry, I'll stop that right now.

I'm not going to tell you how to use this book because I hate it when other books try to tell me how to use books. You turn the pages and read, right? I'm sure you purchased this book for a reason, so I'm confident you know what you're doing here.

But there are a few things I would like to say about what you're about to read. Mostly, it's why I wrote this book the way I did.

I've covered the basics of the entire publishing process from writing, through editing, formatting and of course, publishing. I'm assuming your book is finished and ready to go, but I'm also assuming you're a new writer, meaning the manuscript you're working on now will soon become your debut release. I'm guessing it will need a lot of work and polishing as first books always do (and second, third, fourth books do, too), so I've included some self-editing basics for you. But I'm not going to teach you how to write because that's down to practice. I'll explain some terms and their meanings, though, just in case you're not already familiar.

As you're new to this, I've also assumed you not only want to learn what to do, but keep your costs as low as possible. When I first started I made a LOT of mistakes. I didn't invest in things I should have and I didn't learn as much as I needed to prior to releasing my debut. I probably spent money in the wrong places and on the wrong things. I didn't research as thoroughly as I should have. I hold up my hands and admit it, which is why 'The Soul Sanctuary' (2010) is no longer in print.

So, I've decided to *assume* (there I go again) that you're in the same position I was. I'll show you some free and easy ways to format your book and design your cover professionally, allowing you to avoid the mistakes I made.

Of course, you could just hire someone to do everything for you (like me! Hellooo! *waves*).

Check out the contents page for an overview of what's included and you'll see how I've structured each section. We'll start with the basics, then preparation, then move on to marketing. I hope it's easy to follow and understand. At the back, I've collated a list of useful links for you to use as a quick reference point, too. I'm not into these huge bibliographies and indexes you see in non-fiction books, though, plus I want you to read the whole thing.

Oh, and I've written this in a very 'brain dumpy' kind of way (because 'brain dumpy' is the technical term!). Basically, I've emptied my mind of anything I could think a first-time indie author might need to know, then explained everything for you as well as I can.

You might find it overwhelming and, after a few chapters, decide you can't be arsed with all this fuss. Self-publishing isn't for you, then. Before you go, though, please try to stick with it for a few more chapters, because whilst I'll make this sound like hard work in hell, it's so rewarding and fulfilling knowing your success is down to *you* and you alone.

I decided to write '*The Universe Doesn't Give A Sh*t About Your Book*' for one very important reason: when I started publishing, I wish *I* had a book like this to guide me, honestly, through what it's like to be an indie author. It's bloody hard work, but it's also immense fun. I was so overwhelmed back in 2010 with the various platforms, terminology, rules and laws and opportunities that, to be honest, it was frustrating and sometimes upsetting. I wanted so badly to be a popular writer that I skimped on quality and did things wrong because I didn't know any better; making mistakes, however, is why I'm where I am today. Mistakes made me work harder to fix them, to please my readers and myself.

I don't regret any of them. I'd make those mistakes again in a heartbeat. That's why I'm sharing them with you, so you'll be one step ahead of the E. Rachael Hardcastle I was at 18 (back then I was E. R. Hardcastle, though). Sure, you'll make mistakes of your own and that's fine, too. Then, when you're offering advice to others, you can pay your experiences and successes forward.

Please pay them forward.

"Do you have the courage to bring forth the treasures that are hidden within you?"

Elizabeth Gilbert, Big Magic (2015)

The 'brutal' part of this book is learning about failure and setbacks because we can't all be mega-successful all of the time. Success is in the smallest of goals we meet, in the readers we shake hands with and in the books we sign. Whilst I've tried to write as positively as I can, some chapters may still grind your bones. But, that's just part of self-publishing—we pick ourselves up, dust ourselves off, and crack on.

Another 'brutal' part of this book is in the volume of stuff you should know. I've said it before... I'll say it again: if you don't want to know, you shouldn't be self-publishing. Doing things your own way is different to ignoring the basic requirements, though—the last thing I want is to preach that things must be done a certain way because you will absolutely discover your own methods and hacks. And *that's* OK. Just don't jump in head-first at the shallow end of the pool without your bathing suit on... 'kay?

Finally, you're probably wondering why this book is called '*The* Universe *Doesn't Give A Sh*t About Your Book*'. I have anxiety and OCD—it's no secret. Writing helps with my troubles... my troubles fuel my writing; they've led me to read lots of self-help and personal development books, most of which encourage sending out positive thoughts, energy and vibes into the universe to receive success and the life I want and feel I deserve in return.

Years later, I still have anxiety and OCD...

To some extent, I do believe positive thinking helps us succeed. That's why I practice mindfulness, meditation and yoga. Whilst I expect they will aid my anxiety and leave me feeling inspired and calmer, I *don't* expect them to make my book a bestseller. There is a tiny bit (and I mean tiny!) in the self-care section of this book about positive affirmations, but generally, I think all this 'send out positivity to receive everything you've ever wanted' stuff is mostly BS.

Sorry.

The universe won't reward authors who hit 'publish' and do naff all to sell their book—wishing and hoping it sells isn't enough. **The universe rewards hard work** (though I would argue you reward yourself... after all, *you've* done the work!), so I named my book after the way I *used* to think success would breed.

"A foundation in discipline is always the first step toward victory."

James Scott Bell, *The Art of War for Writers* (2009)

And that's it, really.

With all this in mind, I wish you the very best with your book/s. Write on, I know you can do this!

Rachael x

Publishing Basics: What On Earth Are You Doing?

Welcome to the world of self-publishing. In this chapter, I'll be covering the answers to some common questions and concerns, including:

- *I'm frightened if I publish my book, I won't get any reviews and if I do, what if they suck?*
- *I just want to publish the book so friends and family can read it. I'm not bothered about making money right now.*
- *I didn't even know there was a difference between self-publishing and normal publishing!*
- *I've heard so many horror stories about self-publishing, I'm scared and overwhelmed by what goes on behind the scenes.*

So, to put your mind at ease and start at the very beginning (*a very good place to start...* I know I said I'd stop it but I can't help myself...), let's look at what self-publishing actually is.

What is self-publishing?

Self-publishing (or independent publishing) is when an author publishes their work without the involvement of an established publishing house. The unfinished manuscript you're holding now (and if you're not holding it you're probably looking at it or thinking about it lovingly) can take one of three routes.

There are three types of self-publishing platform you should be aware of before you decide to go indie—four if you include traditional publishing, though it's not indie-related. Sometimes, you can become a 'hybrid' and mix-and-match the platforms you use.

But what are the benefits of self-publishing specifically? Well, if you'd like to keep creative control of your book, set and work to your own deadlines, outsource to professionals of your choice and potentially earn higher royalties, then this could be the option for you.

However, self-publishing doesn't come with the contacts and reach available through traditional publishing, nor does it offer an advance in royalties. It's bloody hard work, and there's a lot to learn.

So, let's start learning...

Four Types

Vanity – when an author pays up-front for publishing services. Vanity press companies can prey on an author's ego, so costs are usually extreme and unrealistic (we're talking thousands). Many authors complain they aren't as involved in the process as they'd like to be or are disappointed with the end product.

I've heard a few horror stories, but I've also heard lots of success stories. It's personal taste, I suppose.

Digital – when an author decides to publish an e-book (or audiobook) only using a platform such as Amazon KDP (Kindle Direct Publishing) or Draft 2 Digital (D2D).

Sometimes shorter books may prove too expensive to

produce as a paperback, so it's easier to release it as an e-book first.

ACX is the Amazon-owned platform for audiobooks.

Print on Demand (POD) – these are the self-publishing platforms that guide you through the process step-by-step and require you to upload your documents to their system, which they then print as/when an order comes in.

Lots of POD platforms are free when you create an account, but some charge when you upload a document. Charges are usually small and reasonable, though.

Traditional Publishing – when the author gains an agent first, who then pitches the book to larger publishing houses which may include the 'big five'. Some houses will accept unsolicited manuscripts direct from the author.

The 'big five' publishing houses are:

1. Macmillan
2. Simon & Schuster
3. Hachette
4. HarperCollins
5. Penguin Random House.

In the past, they were known as the 'big six' before Penguin and Random House merged.

You should judge the benefits of each POD platform against the price—sometimes the free platforms aren't always the best. You will be expected to purchase any copies of the book you'd like to keep for yourself and of course the files you upload should have been edited and fully formatted to meet their specifications. We'll look at editing and formatting later.

Of the types of publishing platform listed above, I'd recommend using POD—I use a combination of POD and digital. Most POD platforms now offer e-book options so you can keep everything in one place, but if you'd like to test a book's popularity or create a free giveaway to help promote a business, then digital might be a good place to start.

Print On Demand vs Offset printing

If you're self-publishing, Print on Demand or POD will be another term you'll hear often. POD is exactly what it says on the label—printing one copy of the book to meet the demand of each customer. For example, if you were to buy one of my fiction books from Amazon, Ingramspark (my printer) would produce one copy and ship that one copy to you to meet that demand. This applies for larger quantities too, for example, 100 or 1,000 books.

Though POD has gained a bad reputation in the self-publishing industry due to poorer quality books being produced —not the fault of the printer, I should add—it prevents wastage and storage fees for books that have been printed in advance, which may not be easy to sell.

Bookshops can frown on this method. Book stores need to know they can easily return books (and gain stock for a reasonable price to begin with), and most POD platforms won't offer sale or return options to the author. However, be advised Ingramspark do.

Offset printing uses large rolls of paper and is used for most mass market paperback books because it offers higher quality and a wider variety of sizes. Usually, there is a minimum number of books you can order (for example, 50 in a batch), so POD isn't an option here.

One of the great things, however, are the choices you're offered, such as gloss or matte cover finishes, embossing, varnishing, or even cloth-bound hardbacks.

It sounds great, but it can be more expensive and upfront investment is required to order in bulk and, of course, you'll need somewhere to store them, which means you're taking that extra risk.

What if you can't sell those books? How will you make back the money?

Audio Books

When a book is read aloud as a recording—either by the author or a voice actor/actress—this is called an audiobook. They are great for people with less time and can be played through most devices. I know plenty of people who listen to them on the train to work or in the gym.

One of the popular audiobook creation platforms is ACX, which is run by Amazon. You may also have heard of Audible, which is a platform for purchasing and listening to them. There are, however, plenty of others available for the creation and purchase of audiobooks.

If your book is being read in full, this will be the 'unabridged' version. If your book is being shortened, this will be the 'abridged' version.

Platform Comparisons

You: *So Rachael, which is the best self-publishing platform?*

Me: *Ooh, that's a difficult question and one I'm not going to answer.*

But I'm not going to leave you wondering, either.

So far in my career, I've used the following self-publishing platforms: Createspace* and KDP (Amazon), Ingramspark, Lulu, Draft2Digital, plus a selection of the e-book platforms such as Kobo and Nook.

*Createspace was an Amazon-owned company and has recently merged with KDP, so this platform is no longer available.

If you're struggling to find the best platform for you, consider the following questions:

- Do they offer e-book options?
- Do they offer a variety of dimensions?
- Can you publish a hardback with them?
- Will they offer a free ISBN?
- Is it free to upload your files?
- Do they allow retailer returns?
- Do they allow you to set a retailer discount?
- Can you give the book away for free?
- Is there a choice of cover finishes and paper qualities/colours?

- Is there a variety of delivery options and printing speeds?
- Is the printer based in your country?
- Can you privately publish your book?

<u>TASKS:</u>

When you have some time, set up an account with a few of the companies and explore their systems in-depth. At this stage, you don't need to complete any of the payment or set-up details, but you can still access their help pages and tools.

Be aware that each platform's features and prices may change, but research should give you an overview of each before you decide which one to use.

Private Publishing

Sometimes we may just want to self-publish a book that only *we* have access to. Perhaps it's a family project or a personal journal you'd like to see in print, but don't want to make available for others to purchase.

That's where private publishing applies, and most POD platforms will allow you to do this.

If you change your mind later, there is usually an option to allow distribution for that particular book and set a price at a later date.

Note, however, that at the time of writing this, KDP does not currently offer this feature unless you are happy to receive books marked 'not for resale' on the cover. Such copies are great if you're passing them on for whatever reason (as it discourages unwanted re-sales).

In summary...

I've probably overwhelmed and terrified you already, but I'm going to continue nevertheless.

Got a headache reading this? Imagine how I feel writing it!

Please don't give up just yet because in the next chapter, we'll discuss some interesting options and issues with self-publishing. And that's where it gets interesting...

Publishing Basics: Step Two – Platform Considerations

In this chapter, I'll walk you through a few of my favourite platforms and some of the optional considerations available to authors through them including returns, discounts and freebies.

Let's start by looking at an interesting e-book platform.

Draft2Digital

Draft2Digital (D2D) is a digital publishing company that allows you to upload and self-publish an e-book.

Their system is quick and easy to use, and they have clear reporting tools to display your sales data. Their handy formatting tools make it easy to create a free interior file, which you can download and export as either a PDF, MOBI or an EPUB file to use in an e-book or a paperback. This means you can use their system to create an interior file and take it elsewhere if necessary.

EPUB – E-book file formats (may not work on Kindle)

MOBI – Amazon Kindle file formats

PDF – 'Portable Document Format'

D2D's system also allows you to publish to a variety of platforms at the same time, and they act as a hub for all your sales data; they'll distribute your book to various companies such as Kobo, Nook, Apple and others for listings through those websites, increasing your reach. Oh, they also distribute to Amazon, too (just be sure you haven't already published that same book with Amazon to avoid duplication).

Another great thing about D2D is you can set a zero price for your book, meaning you can give it away free of charge. Although D2D distribute to Amazon KDP, you'll have to set a price of 99p or above (as Amazon require a minimum price).

Let's take a look at free books now, shall we?

Free Books

A brief note about free books...

I know a lot of you will get asked about free copies from friends, family and colleagues. Some of you may be publishing your book for this purpose alone, though, which is fine too.

First of all, know that you are well within your rights to say no to giving your book away for free—you'll be less likely to be a starving artist. I've found that the more you offer your work and services for free, the more people expect this of you in the long-run. When you start charging, you will lose followers and readers—those who were only there to take advantage of your charity.

Charging for a book or an e-book is no different than charging for a cup of coffee in a café. The barista makes the drink and you pay to consume it. The author creates the story and the reader pays to enjoy it.

So if you want to charge for your book, then charge. Toughen up. Harden your heart. This is business at the end of the day. I set a minimum price of 99p for <u>everything</u>.

Give It Away

Here are some ways to list your book at a zero price, plus some pros and cons:

- Use Draft2Digital, where setting a zero price is acceptable and circulated across a variety of platforms.
- Send the book via e-mail to subscribers as a gift.
- Make the book easily available as a PDF download on your website and through social media.
- Publish the book with a zero price everywhere else (such as through D2D), then ask Amazon to match the price for you. You can contact Amazon through your account and send an e-mail. Alternatively, on the Amazon product page, you can click 'tell us about a lower price' and submit this way. Be patient—it may take a while for this to take effect, but their customer service is always friendly and helpful.
- Run a KDP promotion if you are exclusive to Amazon's platform—they have some great countdown and free giveaway options.
- If you have a paperback edition, KDP allows you to offer the e-book edition free or discounted to anyone who already owns a hard copy.

Benefits

- New readers can try your work without losing money—risk-free, no financial loss and ideal for those who usually only read traditionally published books or have just purchased an e-reader.

- Great for people going on holiday who are browsing the free/discounted content.
- More people are likely to download the book if they don't have to pay for it (possibly) even if they don't read it straight away.
- Less of a piracy temptation. If they can download the book free of charge, there is no reason to unlawfully acquire or distribute it.
- If they enjoyed the first book for free, they may be more likely to pay for the other books in a series. Free books are a great way to hook the reader.
- You will have a shot at getting into the Amazon bestseller list for free books in your genre.
- People may be more likely to leave a review if they downloaded it for free and it was awesome!

Limitations

- You won't earn royalties for those downloads.
- Your book will be easily identifiable as independently published if it's free all the time.
- People may download it and never read it.
- People may be less likely to download the book—if the book is free or of a very low cost, does this suggest the quality is poor or the author is desperate?

Overall, my advice is to offer a free book as a temporary promotion only. The more urgent the offer, the more likely readers are to want to grab it while they can.

Speaking of grabbing a copy...

Stocking Your book

If you'd like to see your book on one of the most popular platforms (for publishing and shopping!) and showing 'in stock' or available for quick delivery, then Amazon KDP is a good place to start.

It's nice to imagine your book will be 'in stock' on the virtual shelves, but if you're using a POD service, it may not always be readily available.

When you publish with KDP, Amazon will list your paperback as showing 'in stock' automatically because it has been published through their platform—one of the benefits of using KDP. Amazon platforms communicate quickly with other Amazon platforms (which is obvious), so you may find any changes you make or new books you publish take effect much faster.

However, when you publish with Ingramspark or other non-Amazon companies who distribute to them, it's common for those paperback books to show something along the lines of either 'out of stock—we don't know if/when this will be available' or 'out of stock—delivery estimated [enter time here].' And, that delivery estimate can be months!

You: *But Rachael, who is going to buy a book they won't receive for three months?*

Me: *Exactly my point.*

When this happened to me, my instinct was to panic. Who would order a book they might never get? When I contacted Amazon, I learnt that once somebody placed an order (proving there was a demand for the book, which makes sense!), it would change to show 'in stock'.

And that's what happened—panic over.

I have since discovered if the book sells well, Amazon may also order stock in advance so your book will show 'in stock', then they may offer discounts on those copies. I logged in to check my reviews one afternoon and saw Amazon were selling one of my books (usually £15.99) at £4.00 per copy. Of course, I freaked out again and contacted them to find out what had happened, concerned I wouldn't receive royalties. I was quickly assured this wouldn't be the case.

Their explanation?

As the book was selling well, Amazon decided to order copies (paying my publisher for them at the price I'd set and therefore paying me the expected royalties per book). As they had the copies, they were then able to sell those on at whatever price they liked. I also realised that Amazon also offer indie books on Prime sometimes (which is free next-day delivery for those who pay for the subscription), so having stock would allow them to fulfil those orders faster, too.

I've advised authors in the past who have seen their books being sold 'second-hand—like new' and panicked. Being new to the publishing game (and that's exactly how it can feel sometimes, like a game), please don't be alarmed if this happens to you.

Most of the time, the process is the same. Whoever is listing your books at a discount will have already ordered and paid for them before being able to advertise them second-hand.

In short, don't worry!

Of course, there is always the possibility the book is genuinely second-hand, which you won't earn royalties for. But still, that's pretty cool, right?

There's a quick and easy solution to listing your books 'in stock' with Amazon. All you need to do is place an order for the book on their website and wait patiently. Regularly search for the book's keywords and the ISBN (International Standard Book Number) daily if you can, so the system registers there is a demand for it. It may take a while for the status of the stock to change, but it will.

If you're not publishing with Amazon, the platform you're using will circulate your book's listing to retailer websites such as Barnes & Noble, Waterstones, Rakuten, Google etc. It's up to these platforms individually if they show your book as 'in stock/available' or not.

Lots of them will recognise the book is independently published and, therefore, will estimate a lengthy delivery to allow for printing and shipping.

At the end of the day, if they don't list your book as 'in stock' and you've tried the above, there's not much else you can do about it (other than publish your book direct through your favourite platforms for a faster listing on their website).

Book Reviews

If your books are on Amazon, you can be confident readers have easy access to the review facilities.

But getting them to leave one can sometimes feel like you're fighting a losing battle. No matter how many times you ask a reader to leave feedback, sometimes they just won't. It's one of the things you can't control no matter how many times you try.

Perhaps they don't know how, or they don't have the time?

Then, of course, the reviews that *do* appear aren't always going to be positive. It can be heartbreaking for a writer to hear negative feedback, but either way, you need to hear it.

There are a few things you can do to increase the odds of receiving a review (positive or negative) and here are my top tips:

- **Include a link in the back of the e-book**, plus a list of your social media handles and website address. If it's right there and just a single click away, it's more tempting. You can also include a 'thank you' page, explaining how readers can support you further if they enjoyed the book.

  - Note, some platforms will reject a book if it references a competitor's details, so it might be worth re-wording it a little.

- **Submit your book to Readers' Favorite** for the chance to receive a free, honest review and a seal for the cover at www.readersfavorite.com.

- **Put a friendly reminder on social media and in newsletters**. 'Calling All Reviewers' is usually how I title these posts, then explain how reviews help independent authors and what their feedback can help you achieve.

  Reviews let you know if you're on the right track, especially if you're writing a sequel. They help to convince other readers to buy the book. I believe in quality, not quantity; I'd be more likely to buy a book with five reviews all voting 4-5* than I would a book with 20 reviews, all 2-3*. Every reader is different, though, and I can't speak for them.

Reviews show the book has been/is being read. They make the book look and sound popular, particularly if the comments are all 'verified purchases'.

And, of course, positive reviews make the author smile!

- **Send out ARCs** and ask those receiving free advanced copies to review the book on release day (with a disclaimer). Similarly, ask your BETA readers to leave reviews (more on BETA readers later). Some platforms allow readers to attach photographs of the book they have received, too.
- **Give the book away for free** for a short period; if people love the book and didn't have to pay anything for it, they might be more likely to leave you some positive feedback. This could also go the other way, though, because if they paid £9.99 for a book and hated it, are they more likely to be annoyed at their loss and leave a disgruntled review?

Occasionally, you may find Amazon remove or delete reviews if they believe them to be fake or posted by someone you know. They rightly do this to ensure all reviews are 100% honest and authentic, so potential buyers can make the best choices. If you share a surname or an address with the reviewer, this might be the cause of the problem.

Amazon isn't the only platform where readers can leave reviews, though. Most retailer websites now allow comments and star ratings. Goodreads (www.goodreads.com) is a community filled with book lovers looking to connect, review and challenge themselves. You'll find plenty of reviews there.

Here's a true story for you:

I was once told that because my books (at the time) did not have many reviews—despite those it did have being 4-5* and extremely positive—that I couldn't be a successful self-publishing coach. My lack of reviews only proved how poor my writing was, *apparently*.

I can't roll my eyes here but as I write this know that I'm rolling them.

This was a comment added to a Facebook feed where I'd offered a struggling author some help. It got me thinking. Despite all your efforts, you can *never* control the actions of your readers no matter how hard you try.

Free will and all that!

Even if a reader thinks your book is the bee's knees, there is no way to force them to leave a review. All we can do is politely ask and make the process as easy and as fast as possible. By constantly reminding and harassing them, you'll quickly lose their custom and will probably never get the review you wanted in the first place.

I feel it's impossible to judge the quality and popularity of a book based solely on the number of reviews it has. Comments and star ratings are super helpful at doing just that and more reviews do evidence more readers, but even *those* books are probably still missing hundreds of potential reviews, as are the bestsellers.

Leaving Reviews

If you're unsure how to leave a review on Amazon, follow these three simple steps:

1. Find the book on Amazon and scroll to the bottom of the product page where the other reviews are displayed. On the left-hand side, there will be a grey button labelled 'write a customer review' beneath the heading, 'review this product'.
2. You will be asked to sign in to your Amazon account. You can still review the book on Amazon even if you did not purchase it there, but do leave a disclaimer to explain why.
3. Leave a star rating and complete the comments box. You can leave your review and even give it a title. Submit the review and within a few days, it should appear.

If you never leave reviews, it would be unfair to get upset if/when others don't leave them for you. I make a point of reviewing every book I finish, even if the book was terrible. If I don't finish it, however, I won't leave one because if I didn't read the whole thing, I can't realistically comment on the quality.

When I do have to leave a negative review, I always start by commenting on what I liked about the book first, then explain what I didn't like. I try to end on a positive if possible so the author doesn't take it personally.

TASK:

Put this book down and find something you've recently read on Amazon (preferably indie, especially if it doesn't have very many at the moment). Go ahead and leave a review. You can even review *this* book if you've read enough of it.

See what I did there?

Verified Purchases & Rules

Verified purchases can be confusing to new indie authors.

If a reader buys your book through the Amazon platform and then leaves a review, *that* review will have a green 'verified purchase' stamp to indicate to other buyers that Amazon did sell that person your book (therefore, it's likely to be genuine).

However, just because a review does not have this marker does not necessarily mean it's not genuine. Lots of people (myself included) who use Amazon a lot will review there regardless of where they bought it. Also, despite it going against Amazon's policies, some authors do still pay for reviews. By reimbursing whomever purchased and read the book, this will generate a 'verified purchase' label.

It's up to you to judge how valuable feedback is. In a nutshell, remember to stick to these rules:

- **Never post or request false reviews** – the comments and star ratings should be an accurate reflection of the buyers' opinions.
- **Keep all reviews free from offensive language**.
- **Be kind and considerate** of the author's feelings. Lots of authors refuse to read their reviews whereas others rely on them for feedback—review other books the way you would want people to review your own. Even if you did not enjoy a book, you can still be polite and reasonable. Provide constructive criticism, not cruel insults.

- **Never pay someone to review your book** as they will feel obliged to leave positive feedback and it will, as I mentioned above, cheat the system.
- People you are close to or who share the same address with you **(family) should not leave a review**. They can always tell you what they thought in person, though.
- Remember that **you can add endorsements and editorial reviews** to an Amazon product page.

  If you publish with KDP, you can use the same login details for your Author Central account. You can also use certain HTML codes to brighten the description, including adding bold, italic and underlined text.

  <b> words go here <b> for bold text is an example of a HTML code. You can Google 'Amazon supported HTML codes' to find tons more information on these!

  Visit www.authorcentral.amazon.co.uk.
- **BETA readers or readers who receive ARCs (Advanced Reader Copies) should state this in their review.** For example, include a line that reads, 'I received this book free of charge in advance of its release in exchange for an honest review.'
- **If you did not buy the book on Amazon but would like to leave a review here, the same applies.** A short disclaimer to state, 'I purchased this book elsewhere but always leave reviews on Amazon' is helpful, but Amazon may still choose to remove it—the reviewer may also have had to spend a certain amount through the website before a review can be posted (quite rightly, too).

Discounting Your Book

A **wholesale discount** is how much of your book's retail price you give to the wholesaler/distributor and retailer. If you use a company such as Ingramspark (like me) you can elect your own. Typically, the more you offer, the wider your distribution may be.

55-50% is fairly standard, and offering this means most stores can safely order the book, sell it at a discounted price and still make money. But, you're giving away half (or more) of your profit here, which for some authors is far too much.

At 40%, most chain stores can comfortably stock the book. If you're targetting online sales, offering 40% won't alienate anyone. Most chain book stores will ask for 40% of royalties from sales anyway, whereas independent stores might ask for 30-35%. Anything less than this and you'd be looking at online sales only.

Most independent publishing platforms such as Ingramspark will automatically calculate your royalties for you when you enter your book's price and the discount you've selected. These estimates make it easier to see if you'll be in profit and if so, by how much.

Returns

Enabling returns allows book stores who order stock to send any unsold copies back, meaning it's less of a risk for them to order in the first place.

We need to make the book as appealing as we can without giving away all our royalties and this is just another way to do that. With Ingramspark, you can opt to have books returned to you if this happens for a small fee.

Pre-Orders

While you're promoting the upcoming release date for your book, wouldn't it be great if readers could order and pay for the book in advance? Pre-orders do exactly this—the book is available for readers to purchase online, claiming their copy early so they don't forget to do so later on!

You're not as popular as the big names *yet*, so every sale at this stage counts. If you're telling someone about the book you're releasing next month, are they likely to remember everything when the book finally releases? Will they have lost that scrap of paper you wrote your details on? Have they been out and bought from another author in the meantime? Are they even still interested? Setting up pre-orders at least one month in advance means any promoting you do beforehand isn't wasted.

Some platforms will expect you to upload the finalised product around seven business days in advance of the release date. They need to be sure what readers are paying for is the finished book. They'll likely send you an e-mail and ask you to check the version they have, then approve it for sale. They may then temporarily prevent access to that book through your account until release day.

Publishing Basics: Step Three – Things You Should Know

Distributors & Wholesalers

You may also be curious about distributors and wholesalers, and what the difference is between the two. These are terms you will come across regularly. Manufacturers (so in our circumstances this would be the printer) deal with distributors, and distributors deal with wholesalers.

A distributor handles orders and holds the stock. They're unlikely to deal directly with the customer due to the size and quantity of the stock they hold, and *that's* where wholesalers come in. They do, sometimes, also sell to retailers direct, however.

A wholesaler will buy from the distributor and sell on terms that have been agreed with a retailer. They'll often buy a large amount of stock (bulk buying) and then offer discounts on those products.

It can sometimes be confusing as some of the companies will do both, for example, Bertrams and Gardeners.

Companies such as Amazon, Waterstones and WHSmiths are booksellers aka retailers.

NaNoWriMo

National Novel Writing Month (NaNoWriMo) takes place every November and challenges authors to write 50,000 words in 30 days or less.

Around this time, you're likely to see authors updating social media to confirm how much they've written so far—sharing pictures and blog posts about preparation and survival.

Whilst NaNoWriMo (and Camp NaNoWriMo) is an awesome challenge, if you're new to writing and publishing, please don't feel obliged to participate right away. If you can't or simply don't want to, it doesn't make you any less of a writer.

If you do decide to brave this challenge, it's a fantastic way to learn writing discipline (1,666 words per day), make some friends and contacts, and it also gives you something to post on social media that isn't 'buy my book'!

Visit www.nanowrimo.org to find out more.

Copyright

Copyright protects your work from being copied and distributed without your permission, and in the UK there is no need to register this with the government.

From creation, a manuscript is protected for the life of the author, plus 50 years. To read more about copyright in the UK, please visit this link: www.gov.uk/copyright.

To show your work has been copyrighted, you will need to include a line to state this in the book itself. Here are two examples of how you can format this:

Copyright 2019 E. Rachael Hardcastle

© 2019 E. Rachael Hardcastle

To insert the copyright symbol in a document, you can press Alt 0169 as a shortcut or access the symbol through your computer's character map.

Copyright in the US works differently. As a general rule, it is usually for the life of the author plus 70 years, though there are other factors to consider. Authors can also submit a form to copyright their material with the United States Copyright Office.

You can download free copyright page templates online fairly easily. Alternatively, open up a book you own and check out how they've structured this page.

First Editions

A first edition is a term used to describe the first 'version' of your book.

You should publish a new edition if you make significant changes to the book's content, such as adding or removing sections or changing the cover. You may have seen 'revised' editions before.

If you produce a book with large print or that is dyslexia friendly, this would count as a new edition, and so would a hardback.

Be aware that different platforms may describe editions differently; their requirements for a new edition and therefore a new ISBN may vary. Generally, if you're just amending the odd spelling or typing error, you don't need to begin a new edition.

International Standard Book Number (ISBN)

An ISBN is 10-13 digits long and can be found on the back of the book near the barcode.

On Amazon, you may have noticed products also have an

ASIN, including e-books. This stands for 'Amazon Standard Identification Number'.

As an independent publishing coach, I'm frequently asked 'should I buy my own ISBN?' and the answer to this question is yes, which is probably not what you want to hear.

While free ISBNs are handy and will save you money, they, unfortunately, offer more limitations than benefits.

When you use a free ISBN, that platform is listed as the publisher of the book. Find a self-published book on Amazon and scroll down to read through the details. Where it states 'publisher', you will notice a company such as Createspace (or any other independent platform) is named rather than the author.

By purchasing your ISBN, you can not only list yourself as the publisher of the book if that's what you want, but you could also enter the details of your own self-publishing company if you have one.

Think about this from a book store's point of view. Most large chain stores will not want to give their money to a competitor so are less likely to order copies of the book if that competitor is listed as the publisher.

Although it still doesn't look as impressive as it would if the publisher shown was one of the big five, listing an independent or small press rather than your name or a competitor means stores may be more likely to order shelf stock.

As awkward as it sounds (because I'm sure you are proud of your self-publishing status), it helps to mask that you're not using a well-known publishing house.

Alternatively, you can use your ISBNs for paperbacks and

hardbacks only. I use Draft2Digital and KDP for e-books and take advantage of the free ISBNs they offer. You can download the Kindle Create programme to your desktop, which allows you to quickly and easily design the interior of your e-book by uploading the paperback document you already have.

Once you've used a variety of their tools and it looks the way you want, you can export the e-book in a Kindle format to make uploading to KDP less of a chore. You can download Kindle Create from Amazon, or simply type it into Google (and it's free!).

By doing this, you can reserve your expensive ISBNs for physical books. And don't worry, Amazon allows you to enter the name of the publisher and will then link the two formats together so your readers can shop conveniently. If this doesn't happen automatically, send them an e-mail and ask. The only downside to doing the above is rather than having one dashboard to check for sales and royalty platforms, you'll have two or three.

Another benefit of using your own ISBN is having access to the details publishers, distributors and potential customers see when they search for your book. If you live in the UK, you'll purchase your ISBN through Nielsen. They ask that you then register with their Title Editor to access your book's listing. Be aware that it can take a few weeks to receive your login information, but once you do, it's a handy tool to have.

Nielsen Title Editor

Nielsen Title Editor allows the author/ publisher to manage their book's data on the database. This includes the title, subtitle, series, ISBN, website, contributors, languages, audiences, reviews and awards, the book cover and more. You can also list the prices and if the book is returnable etc.

It is currently a free service to use, though you can pay for an enhanced service if you wish.

Visit www.nielsentitleeditor.com/titleeditor to register for access to the title editor.

Visit www.nielsenbook.co.uk/isbn-agency to purchase your ISBNs.

Legal Deposits

Something few independent authors in the UK realise is that they are legally required to submit one copy (the most up to date edition/version of their book) to the British Library for cataloguing within one month of publication. This is at the author's/publisher's cost. This means if you publish your debut book on January 1st, you need to send a printed copy of it to the British Library before February 1st.

You should send your book via recorded mail, preferably so somebody has to sign for it and allow plenty of time for them to confirm receipt. It's always a good idea to have a record of the book being sent and safely received. It may take a short while for you to receive an acknowledgement, but a letter will eventually be sent to thank you.

If you're publishing something different such as a magazine or a pamphlet, you may still need to submit. You can visit their website at www.bl.uk for guidelines and further information, but currently, their address is as follows:

Legal Deposit Office, The British Library, Boston Spa, Wetherby, West Yorkshire, LS237BY

Please be aware this may change in the future so you should *always* check online before you post your book. Also, know that other libraries in the UK can request further copies of your work up to 12 months after its release and if this happens, the same rule applies. You must send these at your own cost within one month of the request. These may arrive as a letter or an e-mail, so if you're using a PO Box, be sure to check it regularly to avoid missing them.

You should never assume that your self-publishing platform is sending these on your behalf (they may very well be doing this, but they are unlikely to notify you if/when they do).

The other libraries are as follows:

- Bodleian Libraries University of Oxford
- Cambridge University Library
- The National Library of Scotland
- The National Library of Wales
- The Library of Trinity College Dublin

Category Codes

When you publish a book, you will be asked to select the most relevant categories. For example, you may select Fiction as a general category, then sub-categories of Young Adult and Fantasy. The general advice is to select no more than three.

See BISAC (Book Industry Standards and Communication www.bisg.org/page/BISACEdition) as an example, which is a standard list used by US and English-speaking companies to properly shelve your work at the retailer level.

You wouldn't want your erotic vampire novel being wrongly shelved in middle-grade children's fiction now, would you? That's why it's so important to correctly 'label' your book and its genre so it can be ideally placed for your target audience.

Publishing Basics: Step Four – Take Care of Yourself

Public Liability Insurance

If a third party is injured or something of theirs is damaged while you're at an event or during their visit to your premises, Public liability insurance will cover the cost of any legal action and/or compensation claims they may make.

Most authors have banners up, displayed proudly so passers-by know who they are. But what if one of those fell over and injured someone and they wanted to claim against you or your company? How are you going to pay those fees?

That's where PLI comes in.

Professional Indemnity

Professional indemnity insurance will generally cover any claims against you or your company which arise from breaches of your duty as a professional. If you offer services to others, this is something you may wish to consider. If clients claim for compensation or if you are sued, this would be relevant.

If you do offer services to others, you must protect yourself (and your clients) by using a contract and a waiver of liability. Services such as copy-editing are subjective and different editors will do things in different ways—what is acceptable to one may not be acceptable to another, and authors should know ahead of time that as editors are only human, sometimes errors do slip through.

As a professional, ask that your clients fully read and sign to agree to a contract, which shows they fully understand well in advance what any risks may be. You should, wherever possible, gain a wet signature rather than an electronic one.

I'm not a lawyer or an insurance specialist—please consult a professional if necessary.

Journaling

Other than an excuse to buy a gorgeous journal and a snazzy new pen to write with, personal/private journaling has some amazing benefits.

Writing is a solitary hobby and an even lonelier business if you're running it solo. There are some things you just can't discuss with friends and family; petty complaints you have or self-pity you're feeling (all of which is normal and perfectly OK, by the way!), so it's nice to have a safe, private space where you can dump all this without fear of what others will think. It's like free self-therapy, and I wouldn't be without mine!

I used to journal every night before bed, but due to my busy schedule, I now journal only when I feel I need to. If things get too much—if I have a particularly rough day or come across someone who made my blood boil—I write it down. Then I'm not going to sleep feeling anxious, upset or angry.

You may be wondering why I bothered to include a journaling section in a book about self-publishing.

As an author, the public needs to see the best of you at all times; you should be setting a positive example for your company, fellow indie authors (don't let the side down!) and your readers. People need to feel comfortable talking to you, so being approachable and offering a pleasant smile is a *must* at an event.

If you're worried or stressed, without realising, this can sometimes show in your body language and the way you interact with people. You will seem less invested and interested in what that person has to say because internally, you're worrying about something unrelated. Hey, we all have bad days. You're not expected to be at your best 100% of the time, but your sales will suffer if you don't put in the effort.

Journaling is a great way to empty your mind before and after an event. I'm sure you'll meet people who inspire you, but you may also meet people who grind your bones. By writing this down, you're taking an easy step to being in the ideal frame of mind during and after the event.

Some writers keep a voice journal and record their thoughts on a dictation machine (or an app on their phone) and some express themselves through art.

Your method is your own—there are no right or wrong ways to journal.

> "How much easier is it to lead an unexamined life than to confront yourself on the page?"
>
> Jack Heffron, The Writer's Idea Book (2000)

Success Journal

When I first started taking myself seriously as an authorpreneur (an author/entrepreneur—yes, it's a thing), I religiously checked my social media following every day and, in my 'success journal', noted down my progress to keep track of the increase/decrease, linking this to promotions and events I had running.

Whilst this was good business sense (because we do need to know if the advertisements we're paying for are working) it became addictive. Social media is addictive in general if you ask me.

From 2016, I kept what I called a 'success journal' and completed this every day in a page-a-day format. But, I soon became obsessed with checking the figures, relying purely on numbers to satisfy my need to be successful—if I lost a single follower, I panicked, wondering what I'd done wrong, who they were and if their lack of support made me feel any less of an author.

So, at the end of 2018, I decided to stop and note down my thoughts, feelings and observations as part of my regular personal journaling time. Once a week, I'd check social media to ensure nothing dramatic had changed and any promotions or posts I did share were working, then simply added a few lines to my personal journal entry.

- **Success journal** – a diary purely business-related; a place to keep track of your platforms, express any worries, calculate expenses etc. A safe, private place for you to empty your mind of all things author/success/business-related. *Complete weekly.*
- **Personal journal** – a 'dear diary' style of journaling, where there is no pressure to write anything in particular; the words can flow for as long as they need to and as honestly as I like. *Only I will ever see it*. A place to discuss friends, family, work and other non-business or author-related topics. *Complete daily.*

Try not to worry or obsess over the number of followers, fans and likes you have. You can even do as I eventually did and hide these figures on the platforms that allow it. YouTube is a great example. I can access the figures should I need them, but they are not publicly displayed. Out of sight, out of mind... right?

The trick with a success journal is to make it fun and interesting—you should want to write in it. You can use heart or star-shaped Post-It notes when someone compliments you or your book/s (or provides positive feedback in any way), so on the days you're feeling down, you can flick back and read all the wonderful things people had to say.

Keep track of your sales using a tally, but don't feel bad if those numbers aren't high. Sales can fluctuate for numerous reasons including factors you can't control. But, by keeping this tally for a full year, you can assess which months were more successful for you and thereby (hopefully) why that was.

If you must track a social media platform's growth, focus only on two at a time. I tracked Facebook and Twitter—this bit gets addictive so try to avoid checking more than once per week. If you use a bullet journal like I do, you're probably already used to habit trackers and what they're all about. I'm not going to explain bullet journaling here, but if you're interested and would like to get creative, check out www.bulletjournal.com.

The rest of your journaling space is for your private thoughts. It's also an ideal place to note down contact information for authors you meet, interviewers, reviewers, book store managers, bloggers and anyone in the media.

Positive Affirmations

If your book isn't selling as well as you hoped, it can feel disheartening and disappointing. As a sufferer of anxiety, I often use positive affirmations to re-focus my mind and control unwanted symptoms, so I wanted to share a short paragraph on affirmations with you because they can work equally as well when you're at an event or about to do a reading.

A positive affirmation is a completely positive statement that you can say aloud or to yourself, which starts with the phrase 'I am' and is written in the present tense. Say them when you're feeling worried to help re-program thought patterns, therefore changing the way you feel.

Positive affirmations do *not* replace taking action, though.

Here are some examples:

☹ 'I'm a confident writer who **doesn't** have to **worry** about **not** selling books.'

☺ 'I am a confident, talented writer, capable of selling lots of books.'

The first example is incorrect as it includes negative words. In the second example, I have re-written that same sentence as a correct affirmation.

<u>TASKS:</u>

Write some positive affirmations for the following areas of your writing life:

- Attending events
- Selling your book
- Self-confidence

Preparation: Step One – Editing

Yes, you need to hire an editor.

One of the main manuscript preparation subjects I often discuss with writers is editing. Before you do anything (other than a re-write or reading the darn thing), you should hire a professional editor to look over both the technical issues in the book—for example, spelling and grammar—and the story itself, including characters arcs and subplots.

Character arcs are the inner or physical journeys of a character and the completion of a lesson learnt. This is how the character develops and transforms throughout your story.

I wouldn't recommend editing your book solo. Even if you choose not to hire someone, your book must still be read and checked by *someone*—paid or otherwise—because you're too close to your own project to see it subjectively. The more the merrier.

Chat with a few editors before you hire anyone though; be sure you 'mesh' well and get along—you'll be working closely with this person to iron through something important to you. You need to build a professional, trusting relationship with them. But know that editors don't have to be qualified. They should, however, have a keen eye and, preferably, lots of experience.

Take me, for example. I started editing as a hobby because I found it was something (other than writing) that I was good at, so I took a course. Since then, I've worked freelance, gaining experience and finding regular clients. It's now a key part of my publishing business. Like me, most will offer you a free sample so you can judge for yourself if they're the right fit for your book, and you may be able to pay in instalments. Look for someone with experience in your genre, too.

If you cannot afford to hire a professional, you could ask someone you know to help out. Somebody who works with text every day (an English teacher, for example) would be ideal. Remember that the quality of editing may affect the book's success, so you should never release anything before completing my 6 Read Rule at the very least.

There are two types of editing to consider:

1. **Copy-editing (sometimes written as copy editing) aka line editing** looks at the consistency and accuracy of your manuscript, checking for spelling, grammar and punctuation. This covers what I like to call the 'technical sh*t'.

2. **Developmental editing aka content editing** looks at improving the content and its structure. This includes the story, sub-plots and the characters.

Different editors may offer different services, charging different prices and working in their own way. Remember that editing is a subjective profession; not all editors will fault the same things. What one identifies as an error, another may allow. And although editing can be expensive, it's worth hiring more than one if you can for that exact reason.

Editors can work with either a hard copy of the manuscript (on printed paper) or an electronic document. The latter is preferred because it's much easier and faster—they'll likely use the 'track changes' facility of their word processor. This way, the author can see what an editor has changed and why; both can leave and reply to comments, too.

When it comes to editing, there's still more to consider! Here are three other options:

- **Proofreaders** are usually hired once editor/s have done their job. They are the final professional defence against mistakes.
- **ALPHA readers** are given access to early versions of the manuscript. Their feedback can help to develop the book in its beginning stages.
- **BETA readers** are unpaid volunteers who will read the book for fun and identify any problems they come across. This can be anything from missed grammatical errors to unresolved sub-plots.

Lots of independent authors substitute editors and proofreaders with BETA readers alone, which is a mistake. It's always wise to get a second or third eye before your book goes anywhere near the public—your reputation is at stake, and you could anger a reader who paid good money for a book (and in good faith) if it's filled with lazy, unnecessary errors.

I rarely use alpha readers—I enjoy keeping the initial creation of my books private. But when I approach BETA readers, it's usually after the first copy-editing phase has been completed, when I've had a chance to complete my 'Six Read Rule'. I ask 10-15 different people for their thoughts, ensuring they are within my target audience.

Why is this important, I hear you ask?

There would be no point asking avid science-fiction readers

to comment on your romance novella. It wouldn't interest them. They may not know what to look for. If your book is aimed at both male and female readers, look for anyone with hobbies and reading preferences that are relevant to your genre (for example, children under the age of 12 who like dinosaurs).

Set some clear questions you'd like to be answered, including anything you're worried about. This might be the relationship between two characters or the way you kill the villain at the end. Ask your BETA readers pay close attention to those areas of concern.

Book and Chapter Length

If you've asked yourself one of these questions recently, this short section is for you:

- *Is my book the correct length?*
- *Are my chapters too short?*
- *Should I separate this book into three?*

Books and chapters can be as long as they need to be.

That's pretty much it.

Ideally, a novel needs to be longer than 50,000 words, though some sit at approximately 40,000 and get away with it. Anything less than 70,000 words can be frowned upon, especially if you're writing for an adult.

Think back to NaNoWriMo where we write 50,000 words in 30 days or less.

Sometimes, the length of your book can depend on the genre you're writing and what your readers are expecting for their money. Generally, anything between 80,000-100,000 words is acceptable, but in high/epic fantasy and science-fiction, you can aim higher (100,000+). However, if you're target audience are younger, your count should be lower to meet their needs and abilities.

Pre-school/picture books need only be around 500 words, but middle-grade fiction is perhaps 20,000-50,000 words. Young adult (YA) fiction continues up to approximately 80,000 words.

There are, of course, different types of books to consider outside of genre. You may have heard of terms such as 'novella', 'novelette' and 'flash fiction'. I've found, generally, the lengths for these are as follows:

- **Flash Fiction** – up to 1,000 words
- **Short Story** – up to 7,000 words
- **Novelette** – up to 15,000 words
- **Novella** – up to 40,000 words
- **Novel** – up to 100,000+ words

These figures vary depending on your source, so try Googling the lengths of your favourite books or books in the genre you're writing for a better idea.

One book is a stand-alone, but if you have more than one planned, you're writing a series. Three is a trilogy, and four is a quartet.

Rachael's Six Read Rule

As a copy-editor, it's important to catch as many mistakes in a manuscript as possible. However, authors should self-edit their work thoroughly before sending it to a professional, and that's where my '6 Read Rule' comes in.

I've developed a strategy for new writers to help them cover as many issues as possible in just six rounds of edits. Each round looks at something different.

Self-editing may not only reduce how long it will take for your professional editor to complete their part, but it may also help keep your costs down.

Between each of the following steps, put your manuscript away for 48 hours. By taking a short break from the text, not only can your eyes rest, but you may not grow so weary or bored of repeatedly reading the same thing.

Here is a break-down of my '6 Read Rule':

1. **Plot and character (aka the developmental edit).** Before you do anything else, read your manuscript and be sure your setting, character arcs and motivations, storyline, etc. make sense, are full and complete, clear and concise.
2. **Spelling and grammar.** This round of editing should include UK vs US spellings, homonyms, initial -ing words, pronouns, slang, types of speech, clichés, metaphors and so on. Cover as much of the 'technical sh*t' as you possibly can.
3. **Punctuation and sentence length variation.** Check if your commas can be replaced with semi-colons or em dashes. Have you opened and closed all your speech marks/quotation marks and brackets? Do all your questions have question marks and all your sentences have periods? Also consider your tone, pacing and author's voice at this stage if you can.

4. **Formatting.** You can use Ctrl F to find and replace words in your document. This can aid with the removal of double spacing—you only need one space between a full stop and the capital letter of your next sentence, not two. At this stage, run through your dialogue and be sure you have formatted this correctly. If words are split at the end of a line with a hyphen, keep these to a maximum of four per page.
5. **Accuracy**. Check your facts are accurate and relevant. If you have references, ensure these are all noted and formatted correctly. If you're writing an e-book, do all your hyperlinks work?
6. **Entertainment value.** Read and check your manuscript from a reader's perspective rather than an editor's. Read it in various formats (for example, printed, on-screen and aloud). You could also read sections out of order or even backwards! Is the story entertaining? Are your characters relatable? Did you enjoy it?

The first chapter of your book is likely to need more work because it was the first thing you wrote (while still getting into the flow and feel of your voice). Unfortunately, this is the first thing a reader will see both online and in the shop when they open and sample your book.

Poor editing in a sample or a 'look inside' feature via an online retailer like Amazon can instantly put a reader off purchasing a copy, so take extra care here.

Between finishing your first draft and self-editing your book, put the manuscript away and forget about it for a few weeks. When you return, you will have detached from the project and will see it in a new light.

*Technical Sh*t*

I mentioned above how copy-editing looks at the 'technical sh*t' in your manuscript. The following list by no means includes everything, but it covers the main issues:

- **Spelling**
- **Grammar**
- **Punctuation**
- **Repetition** such as unnecessary uses of the word 'that'.
- **Sentence Length Variation**
- **Redundancies** (aka tautology) are words that repeat the meaning of another word (saying the same thing twice).
- **Pacing**
- **Consistency**
- **Homonyms** are words that sound the same but are spelt differently. An example would be 'their, they're, there'.
- **Choice of Vocabulary**
- **Accuracy**
- **Clichés** are overused phrases. A good example would be, 'cold as ice'.
- **Similes and Metaphors.** In writing, when we say something is *like* something else, this would be a simile. If we say something *is* something else, it's a metaphor.
- **Fillers** are overused words such as 'that', which can often be removed from sentences without changing the

meaning.

- **Slang**
- **Tense**
- **Point of View**
- **Types of Speech** (noun, verb, adjective, adverb etc.)

  A **noun** is a person, thing or place. **Proper nouns** are usually capitalised names, such as 'Rachael' or 'University of Imagination'. **Common nouns** do not need capitalising, such as 'apple'.

  A **verb** is an action such as 'walk'. An **adverb** changes the verb or adjective. 'Emma ran quickly up the stairs.' In this example, 'quickly' is the adverb.

  An **adjective** describes a noun or a pronoun, such as 'hairy'. A **pronoun** is a replacement for a name, so 'he' or 'she' would be an example.

I highly recommend you also research what you need to look for when self-editing your manuscript, particularly the various punctuation marks and how/when to use them.

One of the most frustrating ones is probably the em-dash (—). I'll break down a few others in the next section for you.

Punctuation Problems?

As I mentioned the em-dash above, let's talk about that first.

- An **em-dash (—)** is the width of an 'm' and if often used to replace a comma. When using an em-dash, avoid adding spaces before and after as you would with other punctuation marks '*like—this*' rather than '*like — this*'. The em-dash can also replace parenthesis.

- An **en-dash (–)** is the width of an 'n' and marks ranges or differences, for example, '*2-3*' or '*Leeds-London*'.
- A **hyphen (-)** is the shortest of the three and is used to hyphenate words, such as '*three-dimensional*'.

You can use the handy keyboard shortcut Alt 0151 on your keyboard to insert an em-dash and Alt 0150 for an en-dash.

- Next, let's look at **parenthesis**, also known as brackets. There are three types:

  { } which I call the 'curly ones' are used for sets. You would use them around numbers such as your times tables '*{3,6,9,12}*'.

  ( ) which are the 'normal ones' are those we use most frequently. They add extra information to sentences, for example, '*(even though she promised she would!)*'.

  [ ] which I've named the 'square ones' are used around already bracketed items, such as in equations like '*[(2+2) + (3+5)]*'

- **Semi-colons (;) and colons (:)** are used for different things but are often confused.

  Colons are generally used for lists. '*I went to the store and bought: bananas, apples and pears*.' They can also be used to introduce something, '*He bought me the two things I wanted most of all: books and coffee.*'

  Semi-colons join two sentences and can be used in place of commas or periods when each sentence could also stand on its own. They can be used to separate items in a list (if some of those items already contain commas).

- A **period** (.) is just another word for a full stop.
- **Ellipsis** (...) are three full stops together. You can use them when something is missing, for example, when words have been removed from a quote.

Here is a quick list of punctuation marks for you to reference as/when you need to:

• Comma	,
• Colon	:
• Semi-Colons	;
• Period/Full Stop	.
• Speech Marks	“text”
• Quotation Marks	'text'
• Parentheses/ Brackets	{} [] ()
• Exclamation Mark	!
• Question Mark	?
• En-Dash	–
• Em-Dash	—
• Hyphen	-
• Ellipsis	...

If you'd like to learn about self-editing, try downloading a programme such as Grammarly (which is free with the option to upgrade) and have a read through the errors it highlights in your manuscript. The website is www.grammarly.com.

Alternatively, try Autocrit at www.autocrit.com, which is how I started.

Why not include a round of editing using the above software as part of your self-editing routine? It can't hurt!

Tense & Point of View (POV)

Tense and POV can be tricky, particularly if you switch from one to the other during your story. Be sure these are consistent and that any changes (hopefully done with purpose) are clear.

When writing in **first person**, your text is written from your character's point of view, as if they are telling the story. They would use 'I' a lot, for example, '*I went to the shop*.' This can be limiting as a writer, as you can only tell the reader what is going on in the main character's aka the **protagonist**'s mind.

Second person, however, is where the writer talks to the reader. They will say things like '*you walk to the shop*.' This is used much less often.

In **third person**, that same sentence might say, '*She went to the shop*', so the author tells the reader about a third party. This provides some additional options as the writer can share what other characters are thinking, such as the villain aka the **antagonist**.

Tense is easier to understand. '*I went to the shop*' is **past tense**, because you're explaining what has already happened. '*I am going to the shop*' is **present tense** because it's happening now, whereas '*I will go to the shop*' is **future tense** because it hasn't happened yet.

Active Vs Passive Voice

The best way to explain active and passive voice is by demonstrating it, so here is an example of each:

Active: 'Rachael ate a pizza for dinner.'

Passive: 'For dinner, the pizza was eaten by Rachael.'

Passive voice can weaken your text, though you don't need to avoid using it completely.

In the active example, Rachael is eating the pizza whereas, in the passive example, the pizza is being eaten by Rachael.

Preparation: Step Two – Formatting

Formatting is easy!

First thing's first: the advice in this section is based on Open Office (OO) because it's free and does the same things most other word processors do. If you're just starting and haven't paid for Microsoft Word, try OO.

If you've been writing a while, you might be already using Microsoft Word. Please note that the tools may be in different locations or work in a slightly different way to OO, but the same options should be available.

Although there are is abundance of forums, blogs and videos to help you to format your manuscript, when you're completely new to the process it can be overwhelming attempting to sift and sort through everything.

When I first started as an indie author, I wanted to learn how to do things myself so I had a working knowledge, plus save some cash along the way. I also wanted to know in advance of outsourcing what the job entailed (so I would know if someone tried to rip me off!).

Some authors simply aren't interested and like to **outsource** (hire somebody) to format for them. I'm going to assume in this chapter that you'd like to learn some basics (or else why include it in the book, right?).

What you will need to do first and foremost is check what your publisher's/printer's specifications are. You then have to format to those requirements. This information can be found on their website, usually as a PDF you can download.

You can download and install OO quickly, easily and free of charge. www.www.openoffice.org is their website.

Alternatively, if you're looking for more in-depth software, you can purchase and download Scrivener, which is not only great for writing and planning your book, but also for formatting and exporting in a suitable style.

Visit www.literatureandlatte.com for more information.

Creating Page styles

Although it can be a pain in the arse, it'll save you tons of time and stress later if you set up some page styles in advance. Page styles are types of pages, preset before you begin. In OO, you can create these through 'Styles and Formatting', then by selecting 'Page Styles'.

I recommend you set up two different page styles to begin with. Name one 'normal' and the other 'plain'. To do this, right-click on the 'Page Styles' toolbar and select 'new'.

The **plain style** is self-explanatory; we'll use this on pages where you need nothing but empty space. This style won't even include page numbers, headers or footers.

The **normal style** is for all your other pages (if you're writing fiction). If you're writing non-fiction, you might want to set up a page style per chapter, because this will then allow you to apply a different header and footer for each topic. If you decide to do it, name your styles after the chapters.

Once you've named your first style, you'll need to set up your page. And before you do anything else, select the size of the book.

Some of the more popular **dimensions** are:

- 5x8" Fiction/ Non-Fiction
- 6x9" Fiction/ Non-Fiction
- 8x10" Children's Picture Book
- 4.25"x7" Pocket Size Fiction

My book *Finding Pandora: The Complete Collection* (*2017*) is a 5"x8", whereas *Noah Finn & the Art of Suicide (2017)* is a 4.25"x7". There are a variety of options available, though; check with your printer as some platforms may not offer the full range. This book (*The Universe Doesn't Give A Sh*t About Your Book, First Edition*) is a 6"x9".

Next, you'll need to set your margins. Pick up the nearest book to you and naturally open to any spread. Take note of how you hold the book—the placement of your thumbs, how wide you open it, the text's proximity to the spine, etc.

I usually set my margins to 2cm (inner) then 1.27cm for the others in the list (outer, top, bottom), which is how this book is formatted. This is because I want to ensure the inside text is easy to read without having to bend the spine. I also like to leave the reader space at the outer edges to rest their thumbs without covering any words.

Select a portrait or landscape **orientation** depending on the book you're producing, then choose a 'mirrored' page **layout**. Portrait means the book will be taller rather than wider and landscape layouts are wider and shorter.

Everything else in this section can be ignored.

Once you're happy, you can move on to the **header and footer settings**.

For your normal style (when writing a fiction book), you will need to select 'header on' and 'footer on', but if you plan to have a different heading on the left and right pages for a non-fiction book, untick 'same content left/right'. You can, however, tick this on the 'footer' page because the only thing we'll be putting in the footer will be page numbers.

For your plain style pages, do not select to apply a header or a footer at all. These should be used on the left-hand-side only; preferably, we want all our new chapters to start on the right hand-side.

Applying Page Styles

When it's time to begin a new chapter, move your cursor to the end of the final sentence. Go to 'Insert', then choose 'Manual Break' and select the page style you need from the drop-down list.

If your chapter ends on the right-hand-side, you'll need to select a plain style for the left, then go back to 'Insert', 'Manual Break' again and this time select to insert a normal page style. This will ensure the next chapter starts on the right-hand side and includes a header/footer.

Remember, if you're writing a non-fiction book, you would select the page style that matches the next chapter.

When you insert a new page style, the text can sometimes automatically shift to the next page because of extra line spaces, unseen after your final paragraph. All you need to do is click at the top of the page where you want the text to appear and hit the 'delete' key.

Headers and Footers

If you want to add page numbers (aka **pagination**) within your footers, you can click on 'Insert' then select either the Header or Footer option. Page numbers are important but are sometimes omitted from children's picture books.

To add titles within the headers, you can double click in the boxes and type normally. You can also choose how the text looks (font, size, colour, position, etc.) using the options in your toolbar.

Usually, the title of the book is shown on the left header and the chapter title/section is on the right. You could replace that with the author's name if you're writing fiction, though.

I like to centre the content in my headers and footers. Some writers prefer to sit their page numbers on the outside edges.

Images

If you're paying someone to design/format your interior and cover, this next section probably won't apply to you. It's likely your designer will already have dealt with this part of the publishing process and prepared everything in advance. It's still interesting nevertheless, though, so stick around!

If you're going it alone, I'm going assume in this section that you have a basic working knowledge of photo editing software such as Photoshop, GIMP or even Canva.

An important thing to remember is that when you're inserting images into your manuscript, we need to be sure they are set at 300dpi (dots per inch) or more in a CYMK colour profile. Colour profiles and image quality can be set up and selected in your photo editing software's settings.

When the manuscript is ready, ensure you export it as a 'PDF' or 'PDF for Print' in a one-up format. This means as you scroll through the document, pages should not be side-by-side.

If you're inserting images with a white rather than transparent background, be sure to check you have selected to print on white paper and not cream. Some platforms will limit your options anyway. If you don't, your images will be surrounded by an ugly white box.

Online platforms like Canva and software such as GIMP are a great place to start. Canva is free to use with the option to upgrade for access to some extra tools and benefits. GIMP is also free but needs to be downloaded to your computer. You can visit www.canva.com and www.gimp.org for more information.

Contents Page

To insert a contents page, first ensure you have correctly labelled your headers (heading 1 for titles, headings 2 and 3 for sub-headings). Once you have these formatted, you can click 'insert' and then go to 'indexes and tables'.

You can give the list a title, for example 'Table of Contents', then choose the way you want it to look.

If you're writing a novel, you don't need to include a contents page.

Bleed

So, what on *earth* does 'bleed' mean?

It may sound over-complicated but basically, it's a printing term used to describe content which extends beyond where the book is trimmed—applying mostly when you have images or content that covers the entire page like in a children's picture book. This book, as an example, does not have bleed because there is nothing but white space at the edges.

Imagine I am sliding your book beneath a guillotine—picture large blades coming down on the outside edges to ensure it has a nice, straight finish. CHOP! You have to keep anything important well within those boundaries to prevent it from being cut off.

Bleed is usually an additional 0.125” at the outside edges, top and bottom of the page (not at the inner margin, though).

For books with a coloured interior, some platforms like Ingramspark require a blank space in the margin aka the 'gutter'. You may have selected a 5”x8” trim, which is a term used for the dimensions of the book, with full images across a spread. Any images you import into that document when preparing the spread (without bleed) should be 4.875”x8”. With bleed, consider the additional 0.125”.

A 'spread' is a term used for a pair of facing pages when you open a book—two pages that sit opposite one another.

Be sure to check your last page is blank and your page count is divisible by two. Simply add an additional blank page if necessary.

Finally, it goes without saying that you should read up on your printer's requirements—these may change or differ to the above.

Technical Terms

- **Alignment**: When you see straight text at both sides of a page (like in this book) it's called 'justification'. Straight text on one side but untidy on the other is called 'ragged'.

- When choosing where to start a new chapter, consider the right-hand side of the page. This is called '**recto**'. You may notice this is sometimes opposite a completely blank page on the left which is called '**verso**'.
- **Widows and orphans** unbalance your text. A widow is when the last line of a paragraph at the bottom of a page is left at the top of the next page by itself. An orphan, however, is when the first line of a paragraph is left alone at the bottom of a page, and the rest of the text continues to the next. Sometimes, it's easier to just move a paragraph/section to a new page.
- **Leading** is the space between lines of text.
- **Rivers** are the spaces between words.
- **Kerning** is the adjustment of spaces between certain letters.

The above can be fixed and adjusted in your paragraph settings. Highlight the paragraph you want to amend and right-click, then select 'Paragraph' to access the options.

Dialogue

Formatting dialogue for your debut book can be tricky and confusing. My advice depends entirely on what's being said and who by.

Here are a few examples:

"Hello, Rachael," said John. "How are you today?"

Dialogue usually ends with a comma before the closing speech marks, followed by a lower case action such as 'said'. If what they are saying can be split into two sentences like in the above example, you can use a full stop, then a capital for the start of the next part of the speech.

"Hello, Rachael. How are you today**?"** **s**aid John.

In this second example, we're saying the same thing in a slightly different way. There are still two sentences but they haven't been separated by the writer with action. Although we end with a question mark and not a comma, we still use a lower case s in 'said' because this action relates to the speech it just followed.

"Rachael**,"** **s**aid John**,** **"h**ow are you today?"
"Rachael**,"** **J**ohn said**,** **"h**ow are you today?"

These examples show John is using one single sentence, but the writer has chosen to split it in half with action. Because this is two halves of the same sentence, we can use commas at either side. Remember, names should always be capitalised no matter their placement.

"Rachael!**"** **J**ohn wasn't sure she'd heard him**.** **"**Hey, Rachael!"

The writer, in this next example, has chosen to separate the two sentences with an extended explanation of John's actions. As this is separate to the speech itself, we treat this as we would any other new sentence and punctuate accordingly. However, in the example below, you can see the explanation leads into the second sentence of dialogue, so we use a comma to show this.

"Rachael!" John wasn't sure she'd heard him so he said, "Hey, over here, Rachael!"

If the speaker is then quoting someone else, we would use double speech marks "like this" for the dialogue itself and single quotation marks 'like this' for the quotation within it.

"I met John the other day and he said, 'I'm running so late!' and I agreed and told him to hurry," Emma said.

It doesn't matter which way around you use these, as long as you stick with your choice throughout the manuscript.

Convenience

Before you choose your book's dimensions, consider if the overall **size and weight** will be more of an inconvenience to your reader than appealing. Sure, larger books suggest more value for money and, potentially, a full series or collection if they love the characters. Until they pick up the book and read the first part, how will they know if they want the full series, though?

If the book is heavy (and/or too thick), are they going to want to read it for any length of time if it causes their arms to ache? Will it be too heavy to take in their hand luggage when they travel? Does the extra weight and bulk mean you'll have to increase the price, or that it will be awkward to transport to and from events?

Consider, also, the **margins of the book**. Set these wide enough to allow for a comfortable thumb position on the outer edges (without covering any of the text) and to prevent readers having to crack the spine to see it.

For an adult book, you should use size 12pt font or above to ensure it's large and easy enough to read. You may sometimes get away with size 11pt. Of course, with children's books, you can be more creative, and large print editions might also be beneficial.

Preparation: Step Three – Cover Design

Basics

Before you even think about designing your paperback cover, ensure your manuscript is finished and fully formatted. You need to know the final page count, and therefore spine width and thickness, first. Most platforms will offer a generator tool for you to download a template, which you can then export into design software like GIMP.

You have less than one second to grab a reader's attention when they are shopping online. When people say they don't judge a book by its cover, they're lying (even though the cover may not *consciously* be their main concern).

Star ratings and reviews on covers might look impressive, but they also need to be from someone relevant or exciting, rather than just Amazon reviewer comments and friends' star ratings!

By all means include endorsements and recommendations if you have them, though.

If you're designing your cover yourself, learn the basics of software such as Photoshop or GIMP (a free equivalent). There are tons of free and cheap design tools available, so there is no excuse for a poor cover design. Alternatively, you can purchase pre-made covers which do the job just as well.

Be sure any text on your cover is clear and easy to read even as a thumbnail, but above all, it needs to be suitable for your genre and target audience. Comic Sans on a cover is not acceptable—there are lots of free, fun alternatives that look and feel much more professional. Visit a website such as www.1001fonts.com and browse what they have to offer, ensuring the license is free for commercial use.

Larger images are going to dominate the reader's attention on a book cover and will be the focal point, but you're more likely to grab their attention if it's centred on the page, particularly if it's surrounded by white space. I prefer simpler covers with a main feature in the centre.

Also, think about whether the cover will look good and read well in black and white. Some e-readers won't display images in colour.

Character Covers

If you have a face on the front cover, your reader will naturally follow that person's line of sight, so have them looking at something relevant to set the scene. Characters at the edge of a page should look inwards (because otherwise, they are looking at something the reader cannot see!), and remember that characters on your cover don't have to match their description in the book perfectly. Readers have an imagination and will each picture your characters differently anyway—let them make up their minds and respect their intelligence.

One of my characters in my *Finding Pandora* collection is a young blonde with a small frame and a bubbly personality. I imagined her to be petite and excitable. Despite the description of the character being in the book, a friend admitted a few months after its release that she imagined this character as a sporty redhead. This proves my point—readers will imagine them in their own way for their own reasons.

Dust Jackets

Dust jackets are extra slips of paper which cover the hardback book beneath. They have two flaps which tuck inside the book at the front and back.

Some authors like to include their head shot and a short bio on the back cover or on the rear inside flap. It's also quite common to see the price and blurb on the front inside flap instead of the back. Reviews occasionally replace them.

Your ISBN and barcode should be on the back cover, and your publisher's logo (if you have one) at the base of the spine. Some books display the genre and available formats near the ISBN, too.

Bevelled Edges

Books with bevelled edges have untidy page edges. They can be an aesthetic addition to paperback or hardback editions, and it's a binding technique used to cut the pages into angles. Most POD companies do not offer bevelled edges, but a local printer might.

Series

Books in a series should appear that way; make it clear that those books are by the same author and take place in the same universe. Take a look at your favourite series. You will notice these covers are similar in appearance without being identical.

When listing the book/s with retailers, you can often complete a 'series' field to provide the name and number of the book. This helps the retailer to group them correctly and guide customers to books two, three and four.

Most serialised fiction will include the number of the book at the top of the spine or even on the front cover.

Summary

Most platforms will offer you guidelines when it comes to printing (and they are all different, so if you're using a few, be sure to check each individually!). You can even download templates if this makes life a little easier.

If you're using a company like Ingramspark, you'll need to ensure you're submitting high-quality PDF documents for both your cover and the interior (300 dpi+) and in a CMYK profile, which stands for cyan, magenta, yellow and black.

The number of pages in your book—and whether you've chosen white or cream pages—will determine the thickness, so you should *always* wait to download any templates until after your interior file is ready.

Though full-colour books can be more attractive, particularly if it's for children, black and white is also an option and can reduce the cost. If you're choosing to print in black and white only (excluding the cover) then you'll need to check it looks good by ordering a proof copy before you publish. Upload the e-book version to your e-reader for the same purpose.

Different e-readers work in different ways because they have various features and display options, so you should check those black and white images are still attractive and easy to see both on and off-screen.

If you upload your book to your chosen platform and it gets

rejected, go through their specifications one at a time to ensure you have met their requirements.

- Did you export the document to the correct size?
- Did you use the correct colour profile?
- Are your images the correct resolution (300dpi+)?
- Did you cover the template provided, or have you left space/s?
- Is it the correct format (PDF)?
- Have you embedded your fonts?

Preparation: Step Four – Pricing

Basics

If you price your book too high—higher than the bestseller in your genre, for example—readers may not be willing to invest in an unknown author. Price too low, however, and they could be suspicious the book isn't worth more.

Before you attend a signing or list a book online, remember to do your research.

Ask yourself:

- What are books of the same thickness and dimensions selling for in your genre?
- What's the most you could charge and the least you could charge?

Ask a selection of people from your target audience if after seeing the book in person, would they be prepared to pay the prices you've come up with. Physically holding the book and flicking through it will allow them to judge its worth. Don't expect an accurate response based on photographs or digital mock-ups alone.

Be sure the e-book is cheaper than the paperback, and the paperback is cheaper than the hardback. Some authors only discount by £1 between each, others by more and some by 50%! For example: hardback £19.99, paperback £9.99 and e-book £4.99. This will, again, depend on how thick the book is, if it's in a series and what your printing costs are.

USP

Now it's time to think about what makes your book so special.

- What makes it stand out from the others in the same genre?
- Why should readers buy from *you* and not from other authors in your category?
- When you're at an event, why will customers approach you and not the author sitting next to you; how are you going to stand out and get their attention?

Your answers to these will create your **unique selling point** (USP).

Imagine you're in an elevator with a famous author and they ask, 'so, what's your book about?' You need to have an interesting answer prepared; something you can say before the elevator comes to a halt and you lose them. Your pitch needs to make them want to ride an extra two floors just so they can hear more, so at first it should be clear and concise.

For example, I'll bet the title of this book was part of the reason you bought it. Did it make you smile or laugh? Was it intriguing? Either that or my gorgeous smile on the cover swayed your decision?

No? Moving swiftly on...

But seriously, when we're at an event, my team and I put in the extra effort and go the extra mile. We invest in technology and we decorate and elevate the display so we stand out in the crowd.

TASKS:

Every fish in the publishing pond has a unique scale that allows them to stand out from the others. Think about what your unique scale is and write it down.

Write an elevator pitch for your book and try it on your friends and family.

Calculating Royalties

How To Calculate

You should ask a book store in advance if they are willing to take stock for their shelves if the signing is a success. Let them know this can be on a sale-or-return basis, and the stock can be signed.

If you don't know what 'sale or return' means, it's exactly as it says on the label. If the books don't sell, the store can return them to you. This means they may not pay you in advance for those copies as a refund will be due if they need to send them back, so don't be disappointed if this happens. It's fairly standard and, to be honest, makes perfect business sense.

Some chain book stores have stickers or labels that say 'signed by the author' so customers know in advance they're getting a special edition. If you can get some of those (or even provide them) this would be handy. The same goes for having the price on the back of the book.

Clarify exactly what percentage of the royalties the store expects (most will take 30-40%), and be sure you're still in profit afterwards. Here's a simple calculation* to figure out how much you're making from each sale at a store signing, based on an example where your book costs the customer £6.99 at the checkout and the store is taking 40% of the royalties:

1. Divide £6.99 by 100 to calculate what 1% of your price is. **6.99 / 100 = 0.0699**
2. Times the answer by the book store's percentage (40%).

You may need to round this up/down. **0.0699 x 40 = 2.796 aka £2.80.**

3. Do the same for the remaining percentage (60%), which on the day is your cut. **0.699 x 60= 4.194 aka £4.19.**
4. Adding both these together should equal £6.99, the original price you set for the book. Then you know your calculations are correct.

*In short, your calculation is [cost of your book] / [100] x [royalty percentage].

Now, using your publisher's or printer's online system, figure out how much you are paying to order your stock. Most companies will offer cheaper rates for ordering in bulk (even if only by a few pence), so my advice would be to work this out based on 100 or more copies. Remember to include any handling fees and delivery charges in your total, then divide that by 100 (or however many books you're going to order) to calculate the cost per book.

If the company offers slower printing and shipping rates to keep costs lower, providing you don't need them urgently, go with the basics. This means your profit per book will be higher.

As an example, for 100 books including postage and handling fees, an order might cost you £310.00. For this calculation, that works out at £3.10 per book. **310 / 100 = 3.10.**

You should be making more per book in your 60% than it costs you to have that book printed and shipped to your home address. You need to break even at the very least to make selling and stocking a book with that store worth your time. To figure this out, simply minus the cost per book from the 60% figure you calculated earlier.

4.19 (60%) - 3.10 (cost of production) = 1.09.

That £1.09 is your profit per book. If what you're making in that 60% is *less* than what it costs to produce the book (for example you're paying £3.10 per book but only making £2.80), it wouldn't be worth your time selling with that particular store because you're losing money. That doesn't mean to say you shouldn't stock a small number with them for publicity purposes if that book store is well known or famous, for example, but you should know in advance what you'll earn and why.

When I release a new book, I *always* calculate what I'll make based on 30%, 35%, 40% and 45%. Then, when I'm planning a signing and that store tells me what they'll be taking, I already know if it's a good idea.

Charitable Donations

You should also factor in any donations to charity. If £1.09 is your profit per book (as above) and the charity whose logo you're using on the cover is expecting to receive 50p per sale, your profit is now only 59p. **1.09 – 0.50 = 0.59.**

The use of a logo may increase interest and sales, which is a good thing, but if donating to them means you're making a loss per book, an increase in sales will only cost you money instead. Of course, if you're giving away all your profits to the charity knowingly, then you can ignore what I've just said (and good for you!).

Remember industry costs can change, too. If your printer's prices increase, so will yours. This means you will be paying more per book and you may need to increase your prices to ensure you remain in profit. For this reason, it's a good idea to check and re-calculate regularly. I've fallen victim to this before when I switched to a different platform, so it's something to keep in mind.

Expenses

If you're at an event where you've paid in advance for your stall/ table, that event should not expect to receive royalties for any books you sell that day. This means your profit per book will be higher, but you will need to factor in how much that table has already cost.

As an example, you may sell £150.00 worth of books, and may only have paid £100.00 for them in the first place, meaning you're £50.00 in profit. If you paid £30.00 to hire the table that day, your profit is actually only £20.00.

- Did you have to drive a long way?
- Have you eaten lunch?
- Have you had to stay overnight in a hotel?
- How much did the banner cost you to make?
- How much were your bookmarks and leaflets, your business cards and giveaways?

Before you know it, you're losing money. Keep this in mind when you plan your event and set your prices.

Retailer Discounts

Some independent publishing platforms like Ingramspark will allow you to set a retailer's discount and choose whether to allow returns. Chain book stores will prefer to order books they can return if they are unable to sell them, so I would generally advise selecting yes (if your platform offers this). With regards to the retailer's discount, some will suggest you set this at 55% because it will make the book more attractive to chain stores.

I must disagree.

You should *never* accept lower royalties just because you want to hold off for a chain book store to order your work. The truth is, they may never order your work and unless you visit each of their stores individually and check the shelves, there's no way to find out if they ever did. In the meantime, you may have had 100 orders from Amazon and earned less for those sales because of it. If you had lowered that percentage to 40% sooner, your royalties for those 100 sales would be higher (and book stores can still order copies if they wish!).

The discount you set should be tailored to your book's needs. By this, I mean if you're expecting to sell more e-books through an online retailer like Amazon than in brick-and-mortar stores like Barnes & Noble, your book will still be attractive to those online retailers at 40%, and some may even be able to offer a discount and still make money.

Never assume that because you haven't chosen 55% that nobody will list or stock the book. Some independent book stores may struggle to offer their customers a discount and to make anything worth their effort if you select less than 50%, but it really depends on what your goals are, and what you want from this book.

Keep in mind that most independent books won't sell more than around 250 copies in a lifetime (for that book). Yours might sell more so this is by no means a way to put you off (I love independent publishing for so many reasons!), but it's true.

Surely for those sales, you would like to receive as many of the royalties as you can, so you can use that money to fund another book?

By setting the discount at 55%, you will be paying yourself less. You're the boss of your business, and surely the boss should be on a decent wage?

Attending Events

Organise An Event

Perhaps you're looking to set up an event yourself by e-mail, or at least initiate an event by contacting a local library, school or shop.

There are a few things you should include in your e-mail:

- **Use a professional layout** – write any e-mails as you would write a letter. Be sure to address it to the correct person in the correct department, and spell their name correctly! If the person's name can be used for both a male or female, check which it is so you can correctly refer to them as he/she.
- **Set up your e-mail signature** if you haven't already done so. Your contact information should be included and be clear and easy to read. In Outlook, you can do this through your account settings.

  By 'signature' I'm not referring to a handwritten signature but a typed template, though if you can scan and include your *actual* signature, that's fine too.
- **Why should they help you?** Before you write to anyone, make a list of the benefits to that company/store. Now make a list of the benefits to you. Their benefits should outweigh yours; they need an incentive to host this event with you and must get something from the experience, whether this is an increase in traffic or financial

compensation in the form of sales or otherwise.

However, be sure to include how it will benefit you, too. If you're local, they may be happy to support you because of those reasons. They should know how.

- Can you **donate a free book** to the location? If they can see the quality of your work beforehand and meet you in person, will they be more likely to agree to host an event?

- Your e-mail should **be positive and inviting** and should be thoroughly spell-checked and proofread.

  If you are sending the same e-mail to several people, be sure you check you have changed any reference to a name/company each time. There's nothing worse than receiving an e-mail that isn't addressed to you (besides, it's lazy and rude!).

Here is an example of a standard e-mail I sent a while back to a store. I've amended it slightly to read more like a template for your convenience.

By the way, the response I received to this was positive!

FAO [Manager Name]:

Good Morning,

I'd like to query how I can arrange a book signing with your store, please.

At the moment, I'm working with [names of other stores] to promote my existing books [names of books], however, on [date], I'll be releasing a brand new [genre] book called [name of book], which I'm really excited about.

I have a lot of promotional ideas for my events this year, which will include [plans so far]. For this reason, I'm expecting to have a few busy days. This book is important to me because [reasons/ benefits to you and the store or your community]. If you'd be interested in working with me for the launch, I'd love to arrange a book signing at your store for [date] for a [full or half-day?] visit.

[Name of the store] has also just taken some of my existing books to stock on their shelves; if you're pleased with the number of sales of [name of new book] at the end of the day, I'd be thrilled to leave a few extra signed copies with you, too.

Please feel welcome to contact me at any time via [telephone number and e-mail address] to discuss, and thank you for your time and consideration.

I look forward to hearing from you soon.

Kind Regards,

[Signature]

'FAO' should be in bold, and you should try to learn the person's name rather than simply stating 'FAO Manager'. You can also replace 'your store' on the first line to the name of the shop itself, for example, '...a book signing with The Little Bookshop...'

These are things you will have to double-check before you copy and paste it to anyone else—they personalise the query.

'This book is important to me because' is your prompt to explain why you wrote the book, and why you're promoting it in this way. If you wrote a book about recycling, this would be your opportunity to explain why recycling is important to you and how they can get involved—how will hosting a signing with this store help to spread the word?

Larger stores can be very busy during the working week and some of them will be closed on a weekend. You'll need to be patient; a reply may not appear in your inbox that same day but that's OK—they're not ignoring you.

Usually, I allow 1-2 weeks (10 working days) before I send a polite follow-up e-mail, just to check they did actually receive it. I've had instances in the past where an e-mail was opened by someone who then went on holiday before they had time to respond, so it wasn't seen by other members of staff (or they assumed it was already being dealt with). I've also addressed e-mails to regular contacts who were no longer working at that company (unbeknownst to me), so their e-mails were lost in the system. It took a polite follow-up e-mail or phone call to the store to learn who'd replaced them.

I keep chasers brief and polite. I also offer to call in (if the store is local) at a time suited to them or give them a call as/when they have availability.

If I still don't receive a reply within another two weeks, *then* I assume they are not interested and I move on. Sometimes they'll reply later and take me by surprise. Sometimes, they never respond at all. The trick is not to take their lack of response personally; they will field hundreds of e-mails each week, many of them asking for similar things and, unfortunately, they just can't say yes to everyone.

If they do say yes, be sure to thank them. As the date of the event approaches (seven days beforehand), be sure to send an e-mail or give them a call to check they are still happy for it to go ahead. This is important because although they agreed, it may not have been written on their calendar, they may have double-booked, or something last-minute may have cropped up. Of course, they may also have simply forgotten! You don't want to arrive in room of confused faces and unprepared members of staff. This happened to me once, and it was *awkward*!

Here is an example of an e-mail you might send for this purpose:

FAO [Manager Name]

Good Morning/Afternoon,

I'd just like to confirm for [date] that you are still happy to host a book signing for [name of book] which was released on [date].

Please see attached a poster advertising the event and if you require any other promotional materials, please do not hesitate to contact me. I will be sure to bring the books, a banner, leaflets and bookmarks on the day.

Thank you again and I look forward to seeing you soon.

Kind Regards,

[Signature]

When the event is over, send them another e-mail thanking them for their support and let them know how much you enjoyed it, even if you didn't. Let's not burn any bridges, and remember to always be polite and enthusiastic.

You can attach any invoices to this e-mail, but it should be the last thing you mention.

Here is a short example:

FAO [Manager Name]

Good Morning/Afternoon,

Thank you to [name of store/ person] for hosting my book signing today. I enjoyed the experience and would love to work with you again.

Please see attached an invoice for the books that were sold, as requested.

If you need anything further, please feel welcome to contact me at any time.

Kind Regards,

[Signature]

Proposals

No, not wedding proposals. Event proposals!

If you're including more information about your book or yourself, and are considering putting together a pack for the recipient, here are a few things you might want to consider including:

- **The event isn't just about you and your books.** How can you make this event matter as much to the host as it does to you, and what can *you* do for *them*? Can you help them to raise some funds and attract new customers in some way?
- Will a donations pot make any difference? If you're supporting a local library or a charity, **can you give a percentage of your profit to the cause** and encourage others with spare change to do the same, even if they

don't make a purchase?

- **Advertise well in advance** (months, not weeks!) and send the venue lots of promotional material to make their jobs easier. Let them know how you plan to market the event and, if possible, send along a marketing plan.

- **Can you offer your spare time in exchange** for their help? If you are unable to volunteer at the venue, can you attend other events they are hosting to increase the numbers and show your support?

Here is an example of what your proposal might include:

- A **professional header** with your contact information and logo.

- The **date and time** of the proposed event and low long you require their venue for.

- How much will the event **cost to host** (hopefully nothing) and how much will you charge for entry? Who benefits from these charges?

- **What *is* the event?** What will happen and why? Is there a schedule?

- Why have you chosen their **venue**?

- **Benefits to the venue**/host.

- **Benefits to the author.**

- **How do you plan to promote it?** Will local media be involved? Is the venue expected to notify the media?

- Are there any **special guests** attending?

- **Thank them** and remind them of your contact details and availability.

Sign and hand-deliver this if possible. If not, post or e-mail it. Follow up with a phone call or an e-mail if you don't hear back within two working weeks.

Setting up e-mail signatures

An e-mail signature is a pre-written chunk of text automatically added to a new or reply e-mail. You can add/remove information from the below-recommended content based on what's relevant to you and your company.

If you don't want this to show on all your e-mails (such as to friends and family), be sure to set up a variety of signatures to use at your leisure.

- Your **name**
- Your **role**
- The **company name**
- Your **contact information** including a telephone number, e-mail address and PO Box.
- A link to your **website**
- Your **office hours**—if people don't hear back from you, it makes it easier for them to understand why.

I like to use a splash of colour in my signature to separate it from the rest of the e-mail, or symbols for the contact information. My name and my role/company name are usually in pink because it's one of my favourite colours. Alternatively, you can use bold.

What happens at events...

When it comes to signings and festivals, you'll never really be able to predict your success or estimate how many books you'll sell before you arrive. There are too many uncontrollable factors, though this doesn't mean we shouldn't be well prepared and enthusiastic!

Success is more likely with research and preparation—get plenty of stock, advertise well in advance and, of course, keep your branding clear and consistent. This means if you have a logo, make it visible and if you have a mission statement, make that visible, too (and discuss it openly).

Generating some social media excitement beforehand can't hurt either, but while your product may be top-notch, sales will still rely on how busy the event and/or location is in general; you can't sell 10 books to zero visitors, neither can you sell a product to women if only men attend.

Get to know your customers

Understanding your target audience is important so we can figure out exactly who we're selling to. Think about who you wrote the book/s for and what your ideal reader looks like.

Here are a few of the main questions:

- **Demographics**

  Where do they live?

  Are you their local author?

  Do they live where the book is set?

- **Age**

How old are they?

Is your book too old or too young for their reading level?

Do they have children?

Can your book be read together as a family—can it be passed down to a younger sibling when the customer grows?

- **Needs and preferences**

  Are they shopping for a book to solve a specific need?

  Are you writing a non-fiction or self-help book, maybe in a particular niche?

  What genre do they read?

  Are you writing in a unique or niche genre?

  Do they prefer paperbacks, hardbacks, e-books or audiobooks?

  Are you trying to sell e-books to people without e-readers?

  What formats do you have available?

  Are they even shopping for a book today?

Just being present at an event is not enough to sell the book no matter how beautiful and interesting it is, or how pleasant you are. Don't get me wrong, though, you *must* learn how to speak to people in a friendly, yet professional manner.

Say Hello

People don't like to be sold to. I have crossed the street to avoid a salesperson with a clipboard before. It's annoying and time-consuming, especially when you're heading to your favourite store or are late for your bus.

Approach people with a greeting to gain their attention, but accept some may not return it (or may even go out of their way to avoid and ignore you, maybe even insult you!). Brush any snarly or rude remarks off, then carry on without allowing your smile to waiver or your passion to fizzle.

Remember that you cannot please everyone, nor should you try. If we all enjoyed the same things, the world would be a very boring place. Choose your battles carefully.

Once you've gained someone's attention and are engaged in polite conversation, ask about their genre preferences. You could even ask their name. A person's name is their favourite word and referring to them by the name they provide will show respect. For example, if they tell you their name is Rebecca, avoid calling them 'Becky'. Using their name shows you have great conversational and listening skills.

Get a copy in their hands by offering it to them in a casual way, but continue to speak while doing so because it's harder for them to interrupt you or refuse to take it when you do. Tell them about the storyline or what inspired the theme, leaving the conversation at a natural stopping point; one likely to prompt further questions if you can.

There's still no way to guarantee they won't hand the book back (or refuse to take the book off you in the first place), but if they do take it from you, they'll be more likely to purchase it.

Why is that, exactly?

Well, put yourself in their shoes. Having stopped to speak to someone selling a signed and personalised book in your favourite genre, and willingly taken a copy to flick through from that person (rather than just off an unmanned table), how would giving it back and walking away make you feel?

As the author, you're likely to feel disappointed if a potential customer walks away at the last minute and that's perfectly normal and acceptable. However, it doesn't mean to say it's a permanent rejection. You can always thank them and (if you're prepared), hand them an attractive flyer or a free bookmark in exchange for their time.

Any interest is better than no interest, and by standing at your table they're doing you a favour regardless of whether they buy anything.

If you don't believe me, try this...

Next time you're out shopping with a friend, find something mundane to gasp and point at, preferably high above you on the opposite side of the street so it's not immediately obvious what you're doing. Ask your friend to play along. Soon, you'll notice others around you will stop or look back to see what's so interesting—curiosity gets the better of us and we don't want to miss out.

By standing at your table for a chat, picking up the book or simply reading your banner from a few meters away, they're already generating potential customers by being present. For that, you should be grateful.

Remember that if you ask a customer to take a photo with you for your website or social media, you will make them feel valued. Gain their permission before you post it, though.

If the customer has heard of you before, they'll want to evidence your meeting for friends and family (who may read the book, too). Agree to all photo opportunities and ask that they tag you on social media by giving them a leaflet or business card including this information.

If you have a selfie square or banner featuring a hashtag, that's even better because it does the work for you. They don't need to remember your details because they are already included in the photo. By sharing and talking about this on Facebook, Twitter or otherwise, they're helping to spread the word.

Appearance

I don't know about you, but when I'm heading to an event, everything we've just talked about seems the least of my worries. I'm usually more concerned with small, pointless things. Except, to me, they don't seem so silly at the time.

Here are a few examples:

- **Should you stand at the table?** No, because that would feel too much like you're trying to sell something (even though you are), like you're not an important, bestselling author they should be excited about.
- **Should you sit?** Maybe make them approach as if you're royalty, or is that too professional and will you miss the opportunity to speak to passers-by?
- **Do you take a banner** or allow the book store to use theirs? Would this mean they don't know who you are, or would a branded banner feel more like a 'real' book signing? Without a banner, surely people will be forced to speak to you to find out who you are and what you're selling, right? Or will having to speak to you put some

people off? With a banner, they may not speak to you at all, though!

- **How should you display your books?** If you stack lots together in a nice neat pile, will people be afraid to touch them or think you haven't sold any? If you stack a few carelessly, won't people feel they need to hurry before you run out, or will they think you're unprepared and messy?

Alright. Let me stop you there.

First of all, book signings can be exhausting. I'm exhausted just talking about them.

You'll be needing a chair, believe me. Whether you use it all day or not is irrelevant. Ask for a chair. Wear some comfortable shoes and, if you feel like you're missing sales by sitting down, get up and move around a bit, but avoid being too 'sales-y' (because that's a word now).

Remember, even *I* avoided the lady with the clipboard! It's not a science, merely trial and error. And sure, most popular bestselling authors sit, but they also have long queues managed by store staff and, if they're famous, security. This doesn't apply to you yet. They don't have tons of books and promotional stuff on their table; all they have is a pen because that's all *they* need.

Do what feels comfortable and natural to *you*. Readers may recognise you and if they do, they'll speak to you anyway. Those who don't are going to decide if they want to meet you whether you're standing or sitting, so try not to over-think this.

Speaking from experience, you'll give yourself a headache!

Remember, if a friend or family member offers to help you for the day, accept their company. In a busy store, staff may not be able to watch your things while you take a five-minute toilet break or run to the nearest coffee shop. If the store/location allows it, they may also be able to hand out leaflets or bookmarks to generate some interest on your behalf. Then, you can have the best of both worlds—someone standing and someone sitting. Be sure to thank your volunteer/s and cover their expenses too; it might be a long, tiring day.

As far as your banner is concerned, yes, you'll be needing one of those. People who don't want to risk being sold to or perhaps don't have the time to stand and chat may still pause to read your banner and grab a leaflet.

Your banner needs to include your photo, a brief bio and a picture of the book cover at the very least. I'd also recommend including your web address and social media details because you'll find people will want to Google you before they say hello. You could be famous; why would they want to miss your signing?

Without speaking to you, people can determine if you're worth their time in seconds via their smartphone these days. I know QR codes are fancy and easy to generate (the black and white squares people scan with their phones), but lots of readers won't know what to do with them. In my opinion, just go for something basic.

You can generate QR codes for free. Simply Google, 'Free QR Code Generator'.

If the store has a backing banner and insists you use that, use it and don't argue. You could still politely suggest they place your branded banner in the doorway to attract passers-by, though, and ensure *that* banner has a poster attached that says 'here today only'. Alternatively, you can use an A-frame—the wooden type you see outside cafes with chalk menus or messages on. If you're in a shopping centre or a public place, check these are permitted first.

Displays, in general, are tricky. They'll vary depending on the location and the event itself. If you're in a book store, keep the display simple and in a similar style to other displays around you. Have plenty of stock visible (and not too tidy!) so people aren't afraid to pick up a copy and believe others have been looking, too.

Have your business cards on display in a plastic holder, which most stationary stores will sell for next to nothing. Have bookmarks and/or leaflets at the ready. You may need to change your display if you're not getting much traction; avoid building a barrier between you and the readers with books or display units, because this can feel impersonal and too official.

Perhaps try the following:

- **Have your prices in a plastic A4 display stand** (those where the paper slides between two plastic panes and stands upright at a 90-degree angle). If this doesn't work and you feel knowing the prices before speaking to you puts people off, remove the list and encourage people to chat; this is a great opportunity to share your USP, for example:

  Finding Pandora retails at £15.99 which sounds like a lot until you learn the book includes all four stories in the series. It's £15.99 for four novels. Reading £15.99 at a distance may discourage people from purchasing, but if they knew beforehand about the USP, they may not be so hesitant.

- **Lay your books flat, but have them stacked.** You can build them as you'd see bricks in a wall; try three books wide in a stack of six, then two above those in a stack of five, then one above those in a stack of three. This, of course, will depend on how thick your books are because the stack/s shouldn't be too high.

  People need to see your face and feel like they can approach and chat without having to peer over a barrier. At the front of your stack, have a display copy people can pick up and thumb through. You could also consider using a small plastic book stand to the side of your stack—it doesn't matter if that copy looks used/worn more than the others, but it should still be in relatively good condition.

- **If you have a small amount of a second book left to sell, include these in the display**, especially if that's all you have left. The selling point for these would be 'get them while they last'. If they've sold well—either at that event or previous events—meaning you're down to your last five or six copies—readers may purchase one of those in addition to the book you're promoting in fear of missing out.

If you have more than one book on offer, remember to include bookmarks or leaflets for your other work when you're signing that customer's purchase. Even if they're not interested, if they enjoy the book they've bought and see the quality is high, they might recommend you to a friend who *does* enjoy those other genres.

When you're at a festival, I'd advise approaching your display a little differently. Build it up and back at an angle as you would see in a shop window. Three-dimensional displays with plenty of colour will attract attention, but be sure to sit everything atop a suitable tablecloth (and from experience, check the table is secure first!). There's nothing worse than an old, scratched and/or wobbly table beneath a quality product (especially when everybody else's is sparkly and clean). You can use empty boxes beneath additional cloths to create shelves if you need to, but I'd recommend purchasing some single book stands so your products are held upright and look inviting. Any boxes you do use should be securely stacked, though.

Try to look your best, too. I'm not suggesting you should spend hundreds of pounds on some new clothes and a haircut, but wear something appropriate, clean and attractive. If you're selling a children's book, don't be afraid to wear some brighter colours with prints (or even a costume). If you're writing a book about business and finance, perhaps opt for something a bit more professional (such as a suit, heels and a blouse). Whatever you're writing, you should be approachable and appear to be that subject's guru.

If you're attending an event as a company, uniforms may also be a good idea, or a branded polo shirt to make your employees easily identifiable.

And if you need to (or are asked to) ensure you wear identification.

Stock

For your first (maybe first-ever) event at an unpopular or lesser-known location, I'd advise taking 20 copies. For larger book store events, double it, or for weekend festivals and conferences, double it again (at least!).

If you're already established and have a platform, you will be able to judge if you'll need more. It's always better to have too many than not enough. Also, if you can discount a little, feel free to do so—current fans or interested readers may not want to miss saving some cash, so they'll be more likely to buy from you rather than ordering online (meaning higher royalties if your calculations are correct). Please be mindful that discounting might eat into your profit, though.

"It's not all about the money, I just love what I do and want to enjoy the experience!" I hear you say, and you're right—you should enjoy every minute of every book signing, because you've put your heart and soul into this book and you deserve to soak in the success. I, too, do this job because I'm passionate about writing and independent publishing, and I want to help as many authors as I can to develop their careers. But, *surely* it would be nice to pay a bill with the profits from your creative career?

As I said at the beginning of this chapter, you're never going to be able to predict your success on a day-to-day basis; some of those books may return home with you, and that's OK too.

Author Copies

I've often seen authors on social media asking whether they are allowed to sell on the stock they have ordered from their publishing platform. To confirm, once you have paid for and received any 'author copies', these are yours to do with as you please. Some copies show 'not for resale', so I wouldn't advise selling these on (though you could give them to friends and family). When you order a box of 50 for an event, however, you can absolutely sell these on—that's the whole point of ordering them, right?

Some authors get upset when they see their books being sold second-hand online, too. I see this as a compliment; that person thought it good enough to pass on. Lots of readers don't keep books or re-read them, so it makes sense for them to give them away or sell them.

It's not personal.

Once they own your book, it's up to them what they do with it. It's the same as buying a book in Waterstones and then lending it to a friend to enjoy on your recommendation.

There's also the brutal reality that they simply may not have enjoyed it. You can't please everyone, so don't feel offended. At the end of the day, they still bought it and you still earned royalties, so does it matter?

*Uncontrollable Sh*t*

How well the book sells could rely on an array of external factors including, but not limited to, the following:

- **The weather.** If it's a bright, sunny day, will people be at the park instead? If it's raining heavily, are people staying at home? Alternatively, will it drive them inside to their nearest store? Check the weather beforehand and plan any important events during seasons where the weather works to your advantage.
- If your store has a **coffee shop**, this can potentially increase sales for you too because people love to buy a book, then sit with a brew and flick through it.
- **Other ongoing events.** Are you signing books on the same day as a local festival? Could people be attending that instead? Alternatively, if it's near-by will you

naturally have extra customers because of the increased traffic?

- **Is it a holiday or a special occasion?** Are you selling more today than you will next month because it's Father's Day or Easter? Are you selling more children's books because schools are currently closed for the summer? Is your book about Christmas and you're selling it in December?

- **Is your book set in (or gives information about) the city you're signing in?** Will books about New York sell better in New York than in Spain? If you're an author from London signing a book in London, will the 'local author' label work for you?

- **Was the store prepared for your arrival,** and have they made the effort to assist and promote you? Was their website updated with details of your signing? Have they offered you an ideal place within their store to sign books, put up posters or used a banner of their own? Did they share the event on social media? Did they seem excited to have you there, greet you nicely and shake your hand? It's easy to judge how invested a store is in the event and how well they think your books will do by the way they interact with you.

These points are by no means an excuse for selling fewer copies at an event, but they are factors you need to keep in mind. A chain store may not roll out a red carpet for an unknown independent author's first event—they don't know you and are (like you) unsure how well the book will sell. Be grateful they've welcomed and accepted you and, as I like to say, just go with the flow and make the best of every moment.

Failure

After a full day's work, perhaps you only sold three copies and the store refused to accept any for their shelves. You're feeling disappointed.

- Did you fail?
- Did you let yourself and your book down?
- Did you make a fool of yourself?

Have you heard the saying, 'there's no such thing as bad publicity'? In these circumstances, there isn't. You still sold three copies, and (I hope) took lots of photographs of the display and of you standing proudly outside the store for your website and social media. You need to be associated with their brand because it looks good to potential customers. You gave it your all and you still shook hands with a manager that you may now consider a future contact.

Those images are all over your platform and that's three more people in the world in ownership of something *you* created than there was yesterday.

Some authors make book signings look easy, and they'll brag about how many were sold and how much of a success the entire day was, and you might see their Facebook updates and growl with jealousy because they're making a living from it when you're not.

Don't let their confidence consume you.

The truth is, these authors may not have done as well as they say they did and without seeing an invoice or written evidence, you'll never know for sure if it's all for the sake of publicity; if it's a lie to make them look and feel better, clearly it's working because they have sufficiently pi*sed *you* off!

Don't let passion blind you to this industry's uncomfortable reality; it's not a huge money-making business, yet it's still bloody hard work. That hard work deserves a reward and earning money from what you're doing means you can continue to do it in the future. Without it, how are you going to order your next batch of books or your next box of bookmarks?

One of my first 'big breaks' as the owner of my own independent publishing company was with a popular store in the UK. I'd psyched myself up for weeks after receiving news that the manager was willing to host a signing for the paperbacks I had available at that time (and there were several). I enlisted the help of a volunteer, spent some cash on promoting and marketing materials, and we drove my stock several hours away from where I lived to set up, only to find that due to an admin error, we'd been double-booked with another author who was already doing *really* well.

In the few minutes we were waiting to speak with the manager, at least three of their books sold and the customers all went away with photographs and huge smiles on their faces. This author was a superstar, and I... well, *I* was not.

As we were early and not due to sign until the afternoon, we relaxed knowing by the time we'd eaten lunch, our events would no longer clash and we could part ways. However, we soon learned the other author had decided to extend their signing, which would, therefore, overrun into our slot and force us to re-locate to a less visible area of the store. For the first two hours, we had to watch potential customers walk straight to the main table and hand their money and support to someone else, without even noticing us.

Initially, my thoughts were not of anger or of upset, but merely of disappointment. It wasn't fair. In my mind, I knew this was supposed to be *my* big break and I was an embarrassment to myself and my volunteer. It was supposed to be an event to shine a spotlight solely upon my hard work and dedication to my craft—to my passion and talent. I know now that it's a rather selfish and immature thought, but I'd been really excited and lost a lot of sleep over the preparations, so that's just how I felt.

I embraced it.

Internally, I was a panicking train wreck.

Externally, I screwed on my most confident smile and got stuck in regardless because, when the other author decided to pack up and leave, I wanted to be ready (and to do my best not to cry).

Eventually, they did leave and the manager moved us. For the six hours I spent in that seat, we sold more books than I imagined we would, took plenty of photographs and met some amazing people, including that author (who turned out to be a nice person).

At a signing, try and aim to sell at least four books an hour, which is one book every 15 minutes. That's impressive for an independent author—if you're there between 10am and 4pm (six hours), that's 24 copies!

If you can manage that, you can go home happy.

Working With Others

External Support

Sometimes, it's handy to gain external support from other companies. If you're writing a book about a particular illness and a local charity has offered to allow you the use of their logo for the cover, there are a few important details you need to work out first.

With some charities, you will need to do plenty of research to ensure your book falls in line with their requirements before you publish. A good example of this would be writing for people with Dyslexia—your book should meet certain requirements and parameters before you advertise it as 'Dyslexia friendly'.

Rather than include the logo on the cover itself, it might be wiser to ask for stickers. Then, if at any time they decide not to support you, their logo can easily be removed from any books you haven't yet sold. This will save you having to spend money on a new batch.

Be sure to find out if the company are expecting royalties from sales that are *not* sold in one of their stores. Does having their logo tie you to them in some other way? Do they expect to receive donations per book sold no matter where you sell the book, such as on Amazon?

Either way, clarify how much they are expecting to receive and if you can afford to do this and still make a profit. Sure, their logo may attract more customers and gain more sales, but if you are now making a loss per book, none of that matters.

Don't Rely On Others

This is where I sound miserable.

I once received some great advice (on a personal level rather than a business level) which I think transfers well to the publishing world.

This advice was:

'If you don't expect anything from anyone, you will never feel disappointed or let down.'

This may sound depressing and untrusting. But, when it comes to waiting anxiously for reviews or BETA feedback, remembering this line can quickly ground you to reality; those roles are voluntary and you aren't owed anything.

If they respond late or not at all, there's nothing you can do to fix that. Any reviews or quick responses you do get will be a bonus.

The same goes for book sales. When you publish your book, if you expect to be a multi-millionaire and a famous bestseller, you are likely to be disappointed! However, if you estimate you will sell 100 copies (most of them to family and friends) you may then be pleasantly surprised.

Cancellations

When it comes to dealing with other authors or clients (particularly when you're meeting face-to-face), *always* send a message or an e-mail a few hours beforehand to check they can still make it.

I've unfortunately fallen victim to last-minute cancellations and complete no-shows. As a professional, this can be frustrating, especially if you had to turn others away who needed an appointment.

You may use a diary, but they may not work the same way.

If after two or three attempted meetings you still have no success—they keep cancelling, they never turn up or they are always *ridiculously* late—it may be time to move on. If you're trying to help for free in your own time, consider it their loss and focus your energy and attention elsewhere.

However, if the meeting will result in you getting paid for a service of some kind, then it's up to *you* to make that all-important business decision.

- Do I value my self-respect and time over how much this meeting will pay?
- Is this person taking advantage of me or wasting my time?
- Is it worth the stress and anxiety?

Set a good example. Reply to your e-mails quickly and efficiently, and treat others in the industry the way you hope to be treated. Keep a diary and attend meetings when you say you will. Let people down *only* when you have no other choice (family emergencies etc. can't be avoided, but you can certainly apologise sincerely).

I'd dread to think there's an author out there disappointed in me because of something I said I'd do but haven't done yet. It's about keeping your promises (or not making any in the first place unless you're 100% sure you can keep them).

Marketing: Step One - Websites

Websites act as the hub for your activity as an author. If people want to see the books you have available, upcoming, or find out where they can meet you, they'll Google you and look for a website link.

Your social media platforms should all point to your website and your website should link easily to your social media platforms, whilst also acting as a gallery and a blog/journal where readers can keep up to date with what's going on.

If you can, make your website 'accessible' so it can be easily read from a mobile phone or a tablet. Most design platforms like www.wix.com will offer tools to help you achieve this.

SEO and Keywords

SEO stands for 'Search Engine Optimisation'. Most platforms for web design have the facility for you to make the best of SEO by allowing you to change how (and if) it appears in search engines such as Google.

Wix is a great example, and you can build a free website with them in no time at all.

You may be able to change the title of your page/s and include a brief description of them (which should all include keywords). You may also be able to choose keywords for your website itself, so it's easier for potential customers to find.

You must include relevant keywords so when people are searching for your book or your website, they can find you. While you might think 'books about wizards' is a great keyword for your young adult book about a school of wizards, including that as a key phrase is pointless; an already well-known book dominates those results, leaving yours lost somewhere in the mix.

You can check how many results particular keywords return each month by visiting Google Adwords and typing in a few ideas: www.ads.google.com.

Aim to find 15-20 ideal keywords for each of your books and each of these should have a reasonable score. If it's too low then there aren't enough people searching for that keyword, so it would be a bad idea to use it. However, if your book is in a niche category (something unusual with a specific target audience) then a smaller score may not be such a problem.

If the score is too high (for example 1,200,000) then we're back to what I said about the book about wizards—your entry will be completely lost.

Subscriptions

Some authors like to create a subscription service through their website. Readers and fans can receive automatic updates and freebies in exchange for signing up via e-mail to receive correspondence. This doesn't mean the author has the go-ahead to spam them endlessly with offers, news and invitations, though—stick to no more than three e-mails per month.

Readers should be able to unsubscribe at any time.

On my website, I call this facility my 'tribe', and I'll send out newsletter updates (one or two per month maximum) and if something big happens, I'll send out an update or an invitation to a relevant event.

When people subscribe, they receive a special thank you e-mail with freebies attached. This is in addition to the other e-mails they will receive that month and is a one-off gift.

If you use Wix, you can also set up e-mail notifications. Already subscribed readers will receive an e-mail to tell them when you post something new to your blog. It's a cool, effective marketing tool.

Pages

Here are some pages you might want to consider adding to your website:

- **About** – your author bio and a photograph of you (a professional head shot, not a tacky selfie of you in the bathroom mirror!).
- **Gallery**
- **News**
- **Events**
- **Books** – details of your available book/s and links to buy them. You could also advertise pre-orders here or make use of a countdown clock to generate excitement.
- **Journal**/Blog
- **Contact** – be sure to include your social media links and if you have one, your PO Box address. I would advise against using your home address for obvious reasons.
- **Services** (if these are offered)

- **Testimonials**/Reviews
- **Pop-ups** – on some platforms, you can set up an on-screen pop-up that prompts visitors to subscribe, purchase or review something. Some authors prefer to do this within the first few seconds of visiting a particular page, whereas others like to give people a chance to explore first. These can become annoying and can get in the way, so limit your use of pop-ups and if possible, only display each of them once.
- **Landing pages** – this is a single, condensed page including the information you'd like your reader to see before anything else. This is often part of your website, but inaccessible from the main home page. It's a link you would give out to specific people, for a specific reason, such as offering a giveaway, joining a mailing list or buying a discounted book. You could also share information via a video or a short audio clip.

Try to keep your website as up-to-date as possible—my advice is to log in at least once per week to upload new photos, add event dates, etc.

Domains

Consider purchasing your domain (the name of your website such as erachaelhardcastle.com) rather than using free versions offered through platforms such as Wix or Wordpress (erachaelhardcastle.wix.com as an example).

As a reader, I would feel far more comfortable visiting an attractive, professionally built website with an easy-to-remember domain than a long, complicated one that's years out of date. Wouldn't you?

The free domains are fantastic, however, if you're looking to learn how to use that platform's tools or set up a separate blog.

Purchasing a domain is inexpensive and worth every penny. Choose something relevant to you and if your name is common, add 'author' at the end. Readers need to be able to remember your details and know how to spell them—if they can't find you online for whatever reason, that's one less fan/reader you have.

Example:

erachaelhardcastle

erachaelhardcastleauthor

It's also better to name your website after you as the author rather than your debut book's title. If you produce other books, this may become complicated and the design irrelevant or out of date, particularly if you write across genres. Readers are likely to get fed up of hopping between several websites if you have different domains for different books; it's more convenient to have everything in one place.

Blogs

If you're hoping to learn how to write a blog post from this book then I must apologise. I used to blog often, but soon realised with everything else going on in my life and my workload, I couldn't keep up to posting regularly, which is important if you want to get returning visitors. It works the same as posting content to a YouTube channel if you're giving advice or uploading episodes.

Always better to have a posting schedule!

Whilst I can't advise you about blog posts here, I can advise you to make use of that space to post a monthly newsletter or even interview other authors.

Author Interviews

When I first started writing, I made a point of posting an author interview every week. I'd scout social media groups for writers and would offer to interview independent authors free of charge in exchange for them sharing it with their fans, readers and followers. This would drive traffic to my website and, hopefully, capture new readers of my fiction at the same time.

You should never charge for an interview, but you should make it clear to those taking part what it will be used for and how. I used to send an information sheet first and ask authors to sign to state they had fully read and understood. Included were rules such as 'no bad language or sexual references' and that I reserved the right to edit anything that didn't make sense and remove the interview at any time.

If you do decide to post an interview, read it thoroughly beforehand and approve the content. Be sure it's not offensive and the questions are suitable.

Examples include:

- Why did you become a writer?
- Where do you get your ideas?
- Where do you find inspiration?
- What are your top three marketing tips?
- If you could go back five years and give yourself one piece of advice, what would it be?

Include a link to the author's website/social media in the

interview and a photograph or video (something visual) to make it eye-catching. If you can, you should also include keywords, tags and categories to make it easier for future readers to find.

If you're struggling for website ideas and inspiration, research some of the authors you read regularly and see how theirs are laid out and what content they offer.

TASKS:

Make a list of five websites you like, and then write a few paragraphs detailing why.

Google yourself and see what the results show. Your website should be one of them—how does it look and what would you change about the listing?

Marketing: Step Two - Social Media

Facebook Likes

I don't know about you, but the recent influx in 'like for like' posts in writing Facebook groups has been getting me down.

Don't get me wrong, I can see exactly why this sort of post is appealing to a lot of new writers; the promise of an increase in page likes in exchange for the click of one button seems easy enough.

But, here's what those likes don't do:

- **They don't offer you genuine readers**—the people exchanging these likes are all authors and writers looking to increase their own Facebook page's likes. Just because you have a higher number of likes doesn't mean you have their genuine interest (and they won't become customers).
- **They don't last!** It's easy to hit like on a page and hit unlike one week later. Lots of writers are looking for an increase in likes but will not genuinely like yours in return —a week later (or maybe even a day later) they'll hit unlike quickly and without guilt.

  When you like a page, you begin to see posts from that page and if you're not interested in the content, you either unfollow or unlike to make it go away. What do you think people who 'liked' your page that aren't interested in you or your books will do when your posts begin to appear on their feed?

Exactly.

- **They don't reflect what you believe in.** This sounds daft, but liking a page without reading anything about the person or their books is a mistake.

  What if they write offensive fiction?

  What if every other sentence they write includes a curse word (I know, I know, look at the title of my book!).

  What if they're openly rude to other writers in the group, or all they do 24/7 is post 'buy my book'?

  As an author, you're potentially a public figure and someone who needs to be a positive role model and maintain an image—openly supporting someone that goes against that image (especially if you've done it without realising), can't be good.

By now, I'm sure you're asking how you find people who *will* genuinely like your page, and remain a fan for a long time. There's no magic formula or secret I can give you, but there are a few tips:

1. **Be genuine, be honest, be approachable.** Overall, be a nice person and post relevant, interesting things to your page. You're a writer, so posting a Stephen King quote will interest your followers. Posting a music video with half-naked ladies gyrating over a flashy car is not relevant, and might offend some of your followers. They're with you for a reason, so give them what they signed up for!
2. **Make use of the Facebook page features** including the 'about' section and ensure you link your website (you *do* have a website, *right*?). List events and services and keep

them regularly updated. If you change your prices, update the listing.

Post photographs of you smiling in photographs with your books and at book stores so your readers can see how passionate you are and how much you love your job. This also shows you're active in the business and your community.

When you're releasing a new book, post cover reveals, competitions/polls and Facebook live videos.

3. I don't use **Facebook ads** often but this is another option. I attend a lot of events where I meet people, handing out leaflets and business cards, bookmarks and other marketing materials, which is where I spend my budget for advertising. However, just because you don't use Facebook ads now doesn't mean you can't in the future, so they're something to keep in mind and something lots of authors have had success with.

4. **Post regularly.** Keep your readers up to date with what's going on so they remain interested and your posts remain in their feed. Some authors like to stick to a schedule, or schedule posts to go live on future dates.

The more you ask people to buy your book, the less likely they will be to do so. It's annoying and clogs up their feed; they want interesting news items and fun photos to scroll through on their lunch breaks, not to be bombarded by your begging.

And it's hard not to talk about yourself or your book, I get it. I'm always tempted to add my website link or mention one of my books when I share something that might help people with their project, but that action in itself draws people to you. Although you didn't write what you're sharing, you're making it easy for them to access something useful. You've just done them a favour.

Paid Advertising

Some platforms will allow you to set up paid advertisements or promotions, which they will circulate to your chosen target audience for a fee.

On Facebook, you can narrow the audience down to target specific ages, locations and interests, for example, women aged 30-65+ who read romance and erotica in the UK only. You can access figures for each ad you set up or each post you 'boost', which means you can see if the promotion is working.

You can also tell Facebook what your goal is—do you want people to click a specific link, do you want more page likes? They will automatically calculate how many people you are likely to reach based on how long you run the ad for and what your spending budget is.

Making Friends

In short, my advice is never to accept friend requests from clients (or potential clients) you have never met in person on social media. Posting and commenting in groups to generate some interest and chatting with them via private message or in the feed is fine, but once you accept a friend request, that person can see things on your profile you may wish to keep private. That's why I have two Facebook pages—one is mine for family, friends and colleagues where I post about holidays, days out, etc. The other is my business page @erachaelhardcastle. Here, I post about my books.

Because my comments are usually under my personal

account, I do often get friend requests. I have a friendly system to avoid accepting these and use a template response that I amend depending on the person/query.

It goes a something like this:

[In a private message]:

Hi, thanks for your friend request!

I usually only accept friends and family to my personal account, but I have an author page over at [enter your page link here] where we can talk all things books.

If your request was about one of my services, please feel welcome to reply to this message—I'd love to help you further in any way I can.

You can also check out my company website www.erachaelhardcastle.com and send me an e-mail when you get the chance.

Thanks again!

The same advice goes if you're the person sending the friend request. ALWAYS ask before you do this either in the comments feed or via a private message, because like me, they may not be comfortable accepting a stranger's invite.

If you receive a response like mine, don't be offended. That person has good business and security sense and, to be honest, is likely to be safer to work with than someone who accepts everyone for any reason.

Don't get me wrong, there are some clients I work with who I do have in my friend's list because I've worked with them for so long (and met them in person) that we have a strong enough relationship. There is a degree of trust and understanding. You can judge each case for yourself.

Hashtags

Hashtags on social media are words beginning with the symbol #. They are used to collect posts and information on a particular topic so those interested in that topic can find and read everything related to it easily.

Here are a few of my favourites used across the various platforms of social media:

- #amwriting (sometimes with the genre)
- #authorsofinstagram
- #writerslife
- #writerproblems
- #bookstagram
- #ask (followed by author, agent, editor, etc.)
- #indieauthor
- #amediting

Some authors create their own to promote themselves or their books, or to collect posts about their latest release/s. A few of mine include:

#bluetoothsavestheweb

#ifoundpandora

#savenoahfinn

Finally...

- **Only plug your book once every 10 social media posts.** Provide interesting, free content in the other nine, or followers may get fed up with you.
- If you have an author page on Facebook, **set up an automated response to all private messages**, letting readers know it has been safely received and how soon they can expect a reply.
- **Avoid using bad language** and sexual references unless this is specific to your genre and target audience. If you work in schools, you may find families searching for you on social media, and it would not be appropriate for them to be met with curse words and unsuitable content.
- **Join and participate regularly in groups** on social media, but avoid promoting your website/book via any links unless the rules state you can. If you write non-fiction, commenting and advising others on that specific topic can help readers to see you as a suitable 'guru', which may then lead to book sales or other paid services.
- **Post an 'all about me' or 'all about my book' video** to social media—if you have a YouTube channel, this would be a great place to start. Videos can be played in the background, so it's easier and more convenient for readers to learn about you if they don't have time to read a long blog post. Plus, it's visual—colour and personality make selling yourself and your book much more interesting.
- **Share pictures of your book**. Be sure to smile and hold your book up proudly so readers can see it physically

exists and looks awesome. They can then make a personal connection between your book and your happy face—they'll want to support someone who looks friendly and proud, and will feel they know you a little better.

- **Cover reveals spark excitement.** Consider revealing what the book will look like a few weeks before its release. You could run a giveaway or post the first chapter of the book free of charge on your website/blog to generate some interest.
- **Set up polls** to involve your readers in the creation of the book. If they've contributed, they may be more likely to buy it on release day to see if you listened to their suggestions and feedback.
- Some authors like to run their own **podcasts** or simply appear on other people's to discuss writing and their latest releases. Podcasts are like recorded radio shows that readers can play on-demand and are often serialised.
- Similarly, you can tour blogs relevant to your genre by completing **written interviews** for other people; when they post these interviews on their websites, their readers can then follow links to find and purchase your books.
- When attending events, **make use of Facebook Live videos** and broadcast what's going on to friends and followers. You can then download those videos and upload them to your YouTube channel, website and blog.
- Consider braving the camera to promote your work

through p**ersonal videos or 'vlogs'**. Remember to smile and be positive—readers should be able to relate to you, make that personal connection and build an element of trust.

TASKS:

List at least three social media platforms you've noticed other authors using, but are yet to learn yourself. When you have some spare time, do a little research and consider signing up for an account with these platforms so you can explore their features. Even if you don't intend to post and promote on them, you can still keep your account private, then follow other authors and learn from their content.

Take a look at the platforms you *do* use.

Does your Twitter handle match your Facebook handle? If not, can you change one so it's easier for readers to find you?

Have you updated the 'about me' section of your profile, added a professional photo, listed your services or published titles and linked your website?

Summary

I remember hearing (though I don't know where, sorry!) that buyers need to see a product at least seven times before they make a purchase or click a link.

Can you believe that? Seven times!

Remember, you're a small fish in a huge pond so marketing a book alone isn't going to be easy.

Give yourself a break! Rome wasn't built in a day.

You're not going to become a bestselling author overnight.

These things take blood, sweat and tears but mostly, they take time.

Every fish in this pond has a unique scale that allows them to stand out from the others. How can you identify that scale and use it to your advantage? How can we get the relevant information to our readers *seven times* without spamming or irritating them?

When one of your marketing techniques doesn't work, don't give up. Log your efforts and the response you got, plus why you feel it went that way. Then move on.

There is absolutely no such thing as 'I've tried everything' and when someone tells me this, my answer is always, 'Alright, then I'll be needing a list.'

<u>TASKS:</u>

Decide now what success means to you. Do you want to see your books on the shelves of a popular high street chain store? Do you just want to hold a physical copy in your hands and share it with friends? Do you want to sell 1,000 books in six months?

Start thinking about what success is and means to you at this early stage because it's much easier to measure how well you're doing if you have standards to measure them against.

Set five goals and review them quarterly (four times per year). When you achieve a goal, replace it with a new one and, if you can, increase the difficulty level. If you wanted to sell 50 books in six months and easily achieved that, set your next sales goal at 100 books in three months, as an example.

Marketing: Step Three - Paperwork

Press Releases

A press release gives information on a particular matter and is written as a statement, then issued to the media. There are several sections you need to include in a particular order.

In short, these are:

1. Contact information (this should be at the top)
2. Heading and sub-heading (centred at the top)
3. The location and date (capitals, on the first line)
4. The text body (the content)
5. Any links or calls to action at the end

As an example, here is how you might format your press release for an upcoming book signing based on the above:

COMPANY LOGO

Author Name | Website | E-Mail | Telephone | Address

PRESS RELEASE

LOCAL AUTHOR TO SIGN LATEST RELEASE

ON 1ST JANUARY 2019 1000-1600 HOURS AT [STORE NAME] a popular local author is due to sign her latest release next month... [details about the event].

If you'd like to find out more about the author and any upcoming events near you, please visit [website link].

You can send a press release to local media, book stores and anyone else you feel may want to know about your book's release or related events. Local newspapers and radio stations are a great place to start, and you should attach the press release to an e-mail as a separate document (preferably a PDF), written on headed paper.

Here is an example of an accompanying e-mail:

Good Morning/Afternoon,

Please see an attached press release about [event/s]. These events will celebrate the release of the upcoming book, [name, genre, date of release and name of publishing house if relevant]. Additional dates and interviews may be added and will be listed at [website].

If you would like to arrange an interview or host an event, please feel welcome to contact me on the details below for further information.

Thank you for your consideration.

Kind Regards,

[Signature]

Mission Statements

Your mission statement is an opportunity to outline who you are, what your goals are, your morals, values, ethics, culture, and what you have to offer.

Imagine you're introducing yourself at a public speaking event or someone at a book fair asks about your publishing company. What are you going to tell them? How are you going to squash all the important bits into a short, snappy introduction?

This is something quite personal, so there are no right or wrong answers. You as an individual can have a different mission statement to the company you run.

To get you started, you can use the handy template below. Consider where you would display this statement: social media, your website, your press kit, leaflets and posters.

My name is [name] and I'm a (genre) writer from (country).

I believe that (beliefs) because/so (reasons/ explanation).

My books are (what are they?), which you can find by visiting (website).

I support (what?) because (reason), so I (action).

Press Kits

A press kit is sometimes referred to as a press pack or a media kit, and it's usually a digital set of promotional materials that are distributed (or made readily available online) to book stores, reviewers, the media and more.

Press kits can also be physical, including print-outs, photographs, leaflets, etc., however, these are increasingly less popular because they are costly.

It's important to put together at least a basic press kit so it's easy and convenient for people to find and use the information they may need about you, your book/s and your company. If they have to ask and wait a long time to receive these items, it doesn't inspire much confidence or professionalism!

Here are a few suggested items to include in your press kit:

- **Mission statement and story.** Who are you; what do you do and why do you do it? Include information about anyone else at your company/team with their permission; interviews with these people can make for an interesting read—quotes, too.
- **Facts and figures.** Include your book/author awards, certificates, qualifications, etc.
- **Photographs, logos and print-outs**. You can include bookmark designs, poster and leaflet designs, infographics and head shots here.
- **Product samples.** You could include the first chapter of your new book, an FAQ list, bookmarks, merchandise and more.
- **Press releases, interviews and news.** If you have articles, links and other media involvement, you can include these. You should also include reviews and endorsements of note, plus testimonials.
- **Social media and contact information**.

Marketing Plans

A marketing plan contains a list of things you or your company will do to sell your product (aka your book!). It needs to include a variety of sections such as:

- **Budget**
- **Tactics**
- **Promotions** you are running and discounts you are

offering

- **Sales predictions**—how many are you going to sell and what is this prediction based on?)
- **Publicity**—in-person events and networking
- **Media** and press releases
- **Platform/s** including social media and your website
- **Merchandise** and promotional materials including your press kit, bookmarks and flyers
- **Retailers** and distributors you plan to use and why—what is your reach?
- **Paid advertising** vs free advertising
- **Reviews**/endorsements
- **Joint ventures** and collaborations
- **Affiliates** and sponsors
- **Charities**

It may be a good idea to write your marketing plan in sections; if you're unable to write one per book, then write one which includes as much information as possible about promoting your work in general. You may need to produce one for each genre you write in, because you'll market those in different ways and sell them to different audiences.

Start by including a picture of the book. You can use a 3D mock-up from www.diybookcovers.com and the book's blurb/description and price. Detail who your target audience is and why. How often will you measure how well your book is selling against your strategy, and how do you intend to do this?

Conclude the marketing plan by providing your author head shot and biography, then list your contact information.

Marketing: Step Four - In Print

Bookmarks

The ideal size for a standard, low-cost bookmark is 55x200mm, and these don't need to be two-sided to be effective. Companies such as Stress Free Print can produce these for you—they are of high quality, are delivered quickly and there are tons of options for you to choose from.

It's easier if you design your bookmark in advance, then export it as a PDF and upload it to their website when you're placing your order. You can use Canva to design your bookmark free of charge. Their websites are www.stressfreeprint.co.uk and www.canva.com.

When designing your bookmark, you should include the following details to ensure it's as attractive as possible:

- **Title and subtitle**
- **Author name**
- **Website** and/or social media links
- **Book cover**
- **Publisher** name
- Suitable **images**, colours and fonts for the genre

If you leave the bookmark blank on the back, they can easily be signed with a black marker pen and handed out at events. It will also lower the cost of production.

Leaflets

Leaflets are a great way to market to your readers after an event—it's something for that person to take home after meeting an author to ensure they don't forget who you are and what you write.

It's always better to give leaflets to people who look genuinely interested or who stop to say hello; some readers, particularly if they feel forced to take the leaflet, will simply dispose of it when they are out of sight. This not only wastes your marketing money, but it means you have potentially lost that reader altogether. It's important to pick and choose who you approach when handing out marketing material at an event.

You can use companies such as Vistaprint to produce and deliver batches of leaflets, which should have been created to look as professional as possible. Again, Canva is great for this. A5 is the perfect size. Anything larger, and you'd be moving into poster territory. Visit www.vistaprint.co.uk and check out the options.

Business Cards

Business cards are a must-have for all writers, whether you're published or not, and are approximately 3.5"x2" in size. They should include your name, what you do (aka author/writer) and your contact information.

Most business cards can be printed and delivered at a reasonable price. Companies such as Vistaprint or Banana Print in the UK produce high-quality cards at a reasonable cost. www.banana-print.co.uk is Banana Print's website.

Marketing: Step Five - Common Sense

Business Hours

It may also be useful when dealing with clients who live abroad to add your operating/business hours to your e-mails and your Facebook page. This prevents worry when someone doesn't receive an immediate response. After all, it might be three am for you; you can't answer the phone if you're sleeping!

I work to a strict weekday timetable and I do this to ensure I have some personal and family time, plus time for housework and other responsibilities. On a Saturday, whilst I may not be actively working, I do sometimes field some e-mails and queries if I have time. Sundays are my rest days. Anything that comes in then must wait until Monday.

By informing your clients of your schedule, just like a shop has opening times, they know in advance that a lack of response is not due to ignorance. I also add a line to my standard e-mail signature.

Here is an example of a signature addition:

'Thank you for your e-mail. If this is regarding a service, please allow up to 48 hours for a response during busy periods. I respond to all my e-mails personally and appreciate your patience.'

I pride myself in responding personally to all my e-mails. My clients never receive a standard template response to a quote request or a letter—they get my undivided attention and assistance. Because I don't use an assistant, this can sometimes take a little longer, so I ask for patience (because it'll be worth it).

In future, I may decide to hire a personal assistant to deal with queries, but at the moment I prefer to do this myself.

An auto-response lets the client know if they don't hear from me within 24 hours, I'm not ignoring them; I value their time and trust and will get back to them when I'm physically able to.

If I go on holiday, my current clients are the first to know when I'll be returning so they don't feel abandoned, but I'll also update my e-mail signature and apply an auto-responder and inform new clients that I'm out of the office until further notice.

Consistency

Being consistent across your social media platforms, particularly Facebook, Twitter, Instagram and Youtube, is important. By consistent, I mean use the same profile photo, name/handle and bio wherever possible. If you have a long author name like mine (John Smith vs E. Rachael Hardcastle—so many letters, so little space!) then you can shorten it or use something similar. People need to be able to find you everywhere quickly so they can like, follow and share at their leisure.

For example, my Facebook, Youtube and Instagram are all @erachaelhardcastle, but Twitter is @erhardcastle because I had fewer letters to play with.

If you post to one of your platforms, try posting to the others at the same time. You can link these together so it happens automatically, which can be done through your Facebook page's settings.

Of course, we all prefer one platform over the other and because we only have two hands and one brain, we can't keep track of them all at once.

Nor are you expected to, by the way.

Choose your favourite platforms and stick to updating those as often as you can. Two, maybe. Facebook agrees with me much more than Twitter and Instagram because I've used their platform a lot longer, so the others are sometimes updated less often—I concentrate on those I prefer, where most of my readers are.

However, as the bio/about sections on all of them include my website link, it's not hard to find me elsewhere.

I use YouTube for videos of book signings, events and interviews etc., but purely so I can easily embed them on my website and feature them in my newsletter. Those things are always more interesting with something visual and different included, don't you agree? Nothing worse than pages and pages and *pages* of black, plain text!

Top Tip

'If you don't ask, you don't get'. This is my top marketing tip, and it looks at an author's confidence. We're quite often introverts, and sometimes feel our job is purely to write the book—leave marketing and promoting to the professionals, right?

Wrong.

It only takes a minute to send an e-mail, particularly if you already have handy templates and signatures set up. Scouting for interviews, bloggers and media opportunities doesn't need to be time-consuming. Don't wait to be approached; be confident in your skills and talent enough to approach people and ask for help (free of charge, if this is something they offer).

As an independent, unknown author, you may be waiting a while for others to discover and approach you.

Ask local public figures and businesses to attend your event and/or endorse a book you think they would like. E-mail local bloggers, travel companies or events organisers, or contact them on social media. If they predict lots of people will attend the event, they may even agree to attend themselves because it's an opportunity for them.

Just a few minutes of bravery and confidence could land you, as it did me, a television interview, radio interviews and more.

<u>TASKS:</u>

Make a list of five people or companies that you can think of who may be interested in helping you out for free. Include their contact information and do your research, so when you approach them, it's clear you've made an effort and are genuinely interested.

Take a few extra minutes to think of a few things that may prevent them from saying 'yes', and write what your response would be if this happens. Can you include this information in the original enquiry? When you send that e-mail or letter, resolve those potential issues in the invitation.

For example, if the event is several miles away from where

they are based, can you include a handy bus route/schedule or mention there is plenty of free parking?

Archery

What skills (besides writing) do you have to offer? If you are a creative, well-organised individual with fantastic computer skills, could you offer services to potentially help other struggling writers such as formatting or proofreading?

Evaluate your strengths and weaknesses. Use your strengths as an additional source of income to support your writing.

Identify and own your weaknesses. Nobody is perfect at everything. We all have them—work to improve in these areas before you put those skills to good use too.

A few examples may be:

- Web design
- copy-editing
- Proofreading
- Formatting
- Cover design
- Public speaking
- Workshops
- Reviews

TASKS:

What are you good at? List at least five skills—related to your business or field—that could provide you with an additional source of income while your book sells in the background.

Go ahead and make note of your strengths and weaknesses, too, so you can see where you might need a helping hand.

What are you going to do to increase your skills and deepen your knowledge?

Bestsellers

I'm sure the following questions will have crossed your mind once or twice, particularly if you use Amazon:

- *"Is my book still a bestseller if it reaches number one during a promotion?"*
- *"If a book reaches number one on Amazon during a free giveaway, is it still a 'real' bestseller?"*

The short answer: yes, it still counts.

Some authors may argue against this—if you're not a New York Times bestselling author then it doesn't count, and of course, most of those authors are published traditionally, which makes some indies feel becoming a bestselling author is an unreachable and unrealistic goal.

However, my arguments are all for the above.

Here's why:

1. Amazon is such a huge, popular platform that if you reach number one in their eyes, it's a good indication that your sales are high and generally, there's lots of interest in your work.
2. Despite some niches on the Amazon platform being tiny, therefore having fewer authors in them competing for

number one, reaching number one even in those is an achievement. Some of those categories might include 1,000 authors. Some of them may only include 150. Either way, if you can outsell even 100 other authors, I believe that's something to celebrate (given that most indie books usually only sell around 250 copies, according to a course I took in 2018).

If it's your debut book, try not to worry about how many other authors you outsold. Just be pleased. This is why it's important to get your categories, genres and keywords right when you publish the book, though. It's better to compete for first place in these smaller categories than in 'fiction' as a whole.

3. In my opinion, the bestselling status is about demand and popularity, regardless of the book's price. Sure, it might feel a bit more 'genuine' if you manage to reach number one having sold a hardback book at £15.99 to 150 people in a particular category, meaning 150 people have willingly handed over money in exchange for something you created, but you can still have that feeling of accomplishment with a book on sale, or even free.

Have you ever tried to reach number one by pushing free downloads? It's harder than you think—on Facebook you probably have around 100 friends (not including your followers) and, despite your naïve hopes that every one of your friends and family members will click 'download' if it doesn't cost them anything, you'll be surprised how many will simply scroll past or look, then choose *not* to support you.

It's nothing personal; their lack of participation could be for a variety of reasons including:

- **They saw your post/message at an inconvenient time** and forgot by the time they got home.
- **They don't have an e-reader** or a device that supports similar apps.
- **They genuinely aren't interested** because you were never close—they're in your friend list, but it's so you can both be mutually nosey when it comes to what the other is up to these days. An old school friend or colleague, perhaps.
- **They have 'liked' your page on Facebook but choose not to follow you or receive updates**, meaning they may not have even seen the post.
- **They dislike being 'sold' to**, even if the item you are pushing doesn't cost anything.

  Sending personal messages to people and asking them to do something can be seen as invasive and unsolicited. I know it would annoy me if it happened more than once (twice at a push if it was something I genuinely had interest in).
- **It's not a genre they like or will ever read**, so they see no point in downloading it just to delete it later.

  Maybe it's a waste of time and will lead to you reaching number one without downloads from people who are genuinely invested in your work. Let's face it, sales from strangers always feel more special than sales from close friends, right?
- **Their e-reader is shared and the book is not suitable for others who have access to the device** (such as

children under a certain age).

Here are some other things to consider when you think about your views on the above argument:

- **Do your readers even know the difference between indie or traditionally published book?** Lots of mine didn't until they met me in person and we had a chat about what I do and how I do it. They had no interest in the 'behind the scenes' part of publishing—as long as the book looked good and entertained them, they couldn't care less. A book is a book.
- **Even if they *do* know the difference, do they care?** Anyone not in the industry or familiar with the various publishing platforms may just be looking for something cheap and easy to read. If your book is free, discounted or even full price and is visible to them at the right place and time, would they care that a large publishing house wasn't behind the production?
- **Isn't a '#1' spot on any platform worth celebrating, no matter the logistics of how and why it happened?** Rather than putting other indies down, simply offer a 'congrats' or say nothing at all.

  Don't be the a-hole that publicly questions someone's small achievement/s. I've been the victim of trolls before and while I see such comments at face value and try to ignore them, it does knock your confidence.
- **Are you worried about what other authors will think rather than readers?** It goes without saying that if you're in writing groups on social media platforms like Facebook, you'll have exchanged conversations and

perhaps page likes with other writers, meaning they will be seeing your posts and reading about your success.

So, this links back to the previous three points in this section—rather than worrying how other authors will view your bestselling status (or reading any negative remarks they offer), think about how this will look to readers and other potential fans out there.

A bestselling status looks good, feels good and, in short, **is good**. Be happy and proud of it no matter the circumstances.

I know we can't all agree on the same terms when it comes to what constitutes a 'real' bestselling status, but I'm a firm believer that if someone worked hard to achieve that status, no matter the circumstances, and *they* are proud, then we should support it.

Please, oh please, if you feel their bestselling status isn't 'real', don't publicly discuss this on their social media platform. Not only will it unnecessarily embarrass them and anger them, but it's also unprofessional.

If you do need to voice your concerns, do so in a private message.

Trends

It may also be worth looking at the current trends to judge how well a book will sell at a current place/time.

For a while in fantasy and science-fiction, the popular themes were vampires and werewolves, love triangles, forbidden romances, witches and zombies—but maybe not all in the same book (though I can think of a few!).

By studying past and current trends, it's easier to predict what the next 'big thing' in fiction will be. However, my advice is *always* to write what you enjoy reading, and to write a book you would love to see on the shelf in your local store, rather than to write what's popular.

Can you fill any gaps you feel are missing in fiction? Remember, all ideas have been explored before in some way or another.

When I read a book, I can usually tell if the author didn't enjoy writing it.

Trends change and they do so quickly. Given that independent books can take 12 months to produce, by the time your release date rolls around, people could be reading something else. Purely writing to market may produce unreliable results.

Finally...

- **Donate your books to your local library.** Not only is your book then in circulation within your community, but readers will be pleased to see you're offering copies free of charge to good causes.
- **Run competitions** and giveaways through your website. Give readers a chance to win signed copies of your book/s, merchandise and more.
- **Create some awesome merchandise** such as bookmarks, leaflets, business cards, stickers, pins, balloons, bookplates and clothing. You can also purchase branded USB sticks and other technology.
- **Contact a local school and ask if you can deliver a**

creative writing workshop or a career day to their students free of charge. If they want to do the same the following year, introduce a small fee (because they will know from experience how good you are!).

Be sure to have some giveaways ready for the children such as signed bookmarks, pens or stickers.

- **Share 10 fun facts** about you that readers may not already know. This allows them to build a personal connection with you.
- **Be clear on what you want to achieve from your writing.** It's much easier to reach three clear, concise goals than 10 half-arsed ones!
- **Focus your efforts on your target audience** rather than readers as a whole. Don't try to reach and please everyone because it's impossible. Once you know who you are selling to and why, you can tailor your techniques to best suit their needs.

  Don't spread yourself too thin, either. You'll wear yourself out!
- **Write more books.** The more books you have available, the better. If you're writing in a series, be sure to complete that series so invested readers aren't left disappointed.
- **Do what works, then scrap what doesn't.** Keep in mind, though, that it may not have worked due to timing or approach, so be sure to make notes and re-try at a later date.
- **Leave your business cards, leaflets and bookmarks in**

various places (where you're not going to get in trouble for doing so!). Ask at your favourite restaurants, cafés, coffee shops and stores if they have a notice board you can pin a leaflet or poster to, particularly if you have an event coming up.

- **Write a press release** and send it to local media and independent stores. Local literary festivals may also be interested in working with you.

  Independent Bookshop Week celebrates local stores every year. This may be something you'd like to get involved in. www.indiebookshopweek.org.uk is their website.

- **Can you discount your book** so local indie stores can afford to stock copies and still make money?

- **Gain reviews and endorsements** from local public figures such as radio hosts and celebrities by writing to them and sending a free copy of your book in advance of its release date.

- **Model other success stories**.

  What are popular/successful authors in your genre doing to promote their work?

  Why do you think their marketing styles work for them?

  Is there anything you can adopt and try yourself?

- **Produce free worksheets** and infographics for your website and allow people to download them easily as a PDF or share them with others.

- **Read lots of marketing and business books** to increase

and improve your knowledge and skills.

- **Read books in your genre** as often as you can and examine what makes them so popular.

Getting Paid Securely

If you're not only new to the world of publishing but also technology in general, using your debit or credit card details online may be a cause for concern.

You can Google 'how to tell if a website is secure' and find plenty of information, but generally, take a look at the URL (the web address in the top search bar). If it begins with https rather than http, that sight is secure.

Of course, I'm not an expert and there is always a risk when you enter your details online. Be sure when you do so that you are using your computer so you know who has access and that it is fully password protected. Check to see who is around and avoid using free WIFI to log in to any accounts when you're in a public place.

Paypal is a great alternative to having to input card details all the time, but not all platforms and websites accept Paypal payments. You can create a free Paypal account, then easily transfer money back and forth using an e-mail address.

If you'd like to read more about Paypal, you can visit www.paypal.com.

Of course, most platforms will also send you a payment via a BACS transfer (using your bank account number and sort code) or via a cheque, too.

Only *you* can decide with regards to your payment methods,

and only *you* can decide if a website is to your satisfaction beforehand.

From a marketing perspective (which is the whole point of this final chapter!), Paypal is so common and well-known these days that some readers—if buying directly through your website—will prefer to use this method for convenience and security rather than type in their card number, etc.

If you're transferring a large sum of money, it might also be wise to first transfer £1.00 to ensure it is safely received before you transfer £1,000.00!

My advice is always to receive payment up-front before you supply goods and/or services, even if this is in instalments. Your customer (whether a reader or a client) will want to be sure they won't get ripped off.

I've heard some horror stories from clients and *no wonder* they are so worried about working with someone new! You need to show them working with you will not result in further disappointment.

Just be a decent, honest professional, OK?

As an authorpreneur, you will want to be sure you'll get paid for all your hard work too, which is why instalments are usually a happy medium for all.

For example:

- When editing a large book for an author you have never worked with before, wouldn't it be great if their payments were smaller and paced according to their budget rather than in bulk *before* they've experienced how reliable you are?

- Might this be easier and more convenient for them (and more affordable!)?
- Offering payment plans in smaller up-front instalments means *you* can work on their book and receive payment for it bit by bit, leaving plenty of room to build trust between the parties involved. It also means there is less pressure to meet major deadlines.

And that's it... for now.

Phew, glad *that's* over?

That's probably all you can take for now.

Self-publishing seems easy on the surface but when you dig a little deeper, there's a lot to consider.

Try not to worry—there's absolutely no rush to publish your book. That's the great thing about being an indie; you can set your own deadlines, negotiate your own fees and perhaps even design your own covers and interior if you have the skills.

It should first and foremost be fun and enjoyable, particularly if the book you're writing isn't heading for the shelves but is, instead, for your own benefit.

The contents of this book are by no means the extent of self-publishing, nor my knowledge on the subject, but it's a bloody good start and to be honest, it's *plenty* for you to consider if you're new to the publishing world.

This sh*t is overwhelming, right?

By all means, get stuck into your research and ask around; speaking to other authors and people who have already made mistakes and had to fix them will help you to avoid them yourself. Get a variety of opinions and hear as many horror stories as you can handle.

Self-publishing has a bad reputation because of books considered part of the 'slush pile', meaning unedited with poor covers and zero marketing. They let the side down and we need to prove that going indie doesn't mean publishing inferior work.

For this reason, do your absolute best to produce a top-quality, professional product. It should stand proud beside a traditionally published book—readers shouldn't be able to tell the difference.

If this was indeed too much for you, don't be afraid to ask for help or to outsource work to a professional.

We all have our limits; there is no shame in knowing them.

Of course, if you can be a 'hybrid' author and experience both sides (indie and traditional), that would be equally as awesome! Both routes have their merits and their let-downs, but until you experience each platform and publishing method, you won't be able to say for sure which is the best for you and your books.

- Which did you prefer?
- Which made you more money?
- Which gave you peace of mind?
- Which allowed creative freedom?
- Which met your expected level of involvement?

We are all different—our work has individual needs and you as a writer will find a natural path; one you're confident walking. This being the case, if after reading this book you decide self-publishing isn't for you, I won't be offended (and I'm confident you're therefore making the right decision).

If you want brutal honesty, the self-publishing game isn't for everyone. In my opinion, some books should not have been released. It's never too late to fix mistakes—I learnt the hard way and heck, there are probably still typos in this book despite all the work that went into it and all the people who were involved (thanks again, everyone!).

My mantra is still: '*If you're going to do it, might as well do it right*'.

It's a shame when authors cut corners because these books have such potential. Because the authors rushed, those stories may never see the success they deserve.

One final note...

As we part ways, I'll leave you with the following:

The universe may not give a sh*t about your book, but *you* do. At this early stage, that's what's important, because with the right approach and preparation, we can encourage others to care in time, too.

You *can* do this. I know you can.

You're not alone.

I've had my fair share of one star reviews, trolly comments from self-involved a-holes (some have never written or even *read* a book in their life!) and I've wanted to throw my failures and mistakes out the window only to give them a good kick around the garden.

You're allowed the occasional tantrum—my gift to you.

Now get out there and publish your book—leave an inspiring mark on the world. Voice your truth, tell your story and love what you do.

From the bottom of my heart, I wish you every success.

Rachael x

Helpful Resources

- www.indiebookshopweek.org.uk - Independent Bookshop Week
- www.nanowrimo.org – National Novel Writing Month
- www.banana-print.co.uk – Banana Print
- www.stressfreeprint.co.uk – Stress Free Print
- www.vistaprint.co.uk - Vistaprint
- www.canva.com – Canva (graphic design)
- www.authorcentral.amazon.co.uk - Amazon Author Central
- www.readersfavorite.com - Readers' Favorite
- www.diybookcovers.com - DIY Book Covers
- www.bl.uk – British Library
- www.gimp.org - GIMP
- www.1001fonts.com - 1001 Fonts
- www.goodreads.com – Goodreads (reviews and social)
- www.gov.uk/copyright – Copyright Information (UK)
- www.nielsentitleeditor.com/titleeditor – Title Editor (Nielsen) and www.nielsenbook.co.uk/isbn-agency – Nielsen ISBN purchasing
- www.bisg.org/page/BISACEdition – BISAC codes

- www.openoffice.org - Open Office
- www.ads.google.com/intl/en_uk/home - Google Ad Words
- www.paypal.com – Paypal
- www.grammarly.com – Grammarly
- www.autocrit.com – Autocrit
- www.literatureandlatte.com – Scrivener
- www.bulletjournal.com – Bullet Journaling

Acknowledgements

I won't go on and on here, because those who deserve a thank you already know how awesome they are. ☺

Firstly, thank you to those who edited and BETA read this book for me—I really value your feedback and appreciate the time you took to help me iron through. To Sophie Miller, Petra Van Der Ploeg, Malcolm Clarke, Edwin Rydberg and Andy Pedder—thank you!

To the authors who inspired me to write and self-publish; those whose books sit proudly on my shelf, offering wisdom and inspiration when I need it the most.

To the authors currently signed to my imprint: Pamela A. Pedder, Peter Kay, Kier Jay McGuinness, Carol Martin and, of course, my father and co-author, David Hardcastle. You have made 2019 an incredible year for me, and I hope to do you proud. I'm lucky to have such hard-working, dedicated writers with me.

To my family and friends for their constant support and encouragement. To any of you who kindly volunteered for 'Mascot Duty' and made complete fools of yourselves for the day (anything to sell books!), my aunt Denise Campbell, Bex Marshall, Emily Miller, Chris Wilson and my mum, Dawn Hardcastle.

And to my readers for buying and reading the book. I hope you found my ramblings useful!

*You should give a sh*t about this coupon!*

My wonderful readers... if you're still struggling or have further questions, please don't worry.

It's OK to ask for help. So give *me* a shout!

You can get in touch via *www.erachaelhardcastle.com* or via any of my social media platforms.

Quote **UNIVERSE2019** when you do to claim a readers-only 10% coupon, which can be applied to **any** of my author services.

The coupon is valid only once and time restrictions may apply, so be sure to check the website for details.

About the Author

E. Rachael Hardcastle (or just Rachael), is an Amazon international #1 bestselling author from the UK. She's also a trained copy-editor and a publishing coach with a diploma in Successful Self-publishing. Rachael is now proud to also be accepting manuscript submissions through her imprint, Curious Cat Books.

If you need help with your book—perhaps you're not sure what independent publishing is all about, or you're feeling overwhelmed—you've certainly come to the right place!

Rachael supports other writers by offering professional services including copy-editing, formatting and coaching. Whether you're already an established author or you're just starting out, Rachael can help, and you should know you're not alone on your journey to success.

Rachael absolutely loves her job, and believes that through writing we face our darkest fears, explore infinite new worlds and realise our true purpose. She's here to help you figure out what that creative purpose is.

Personally, she writes to share important morals and values with the world (and of course hopes to entertain some readers along the way with both memorable and meaningful stories).

You can read more about Rachael, her company and her services by visiting www.erachaelhardcastle.com.

Notes...

Lightning Source UK Ltd.
Milton Keynes UK
UKHW012039230620
365480UK00004B/16/J

9 781999 968847